ULSTER & THE LORDS OF THE NORTH

Michael Sheane

Printed in Great Britain for the publishers Highfield Press, 15 Highfield Street, Bredbury, Stockport, Cheshire by B.M.W. Offset Lithography, 34 Northgate Road, Stockport, Cheshire.

ULSTER & THE LORDS OF THE NORTH

About the Author

MICHAEL STEVEN SHEANE. Born 1947 in England. He was educated at Protestant and Catholic schools in Ulster and at the university of Dublin, Trinity College in the Republic. He has been living in England for eleven years where he is in business. His previous books include, *Ulster & Its Future After the Troubles* (1977), *Ulster & The German Solution* (1978), which was a study in federalism, and *Ulster & The British Connection* (1979), set at the time of Home Rule. His books are read internationally, and he contributes to radio on Ulster affairs.

CONTENTS

IRISH HISTORY: TIME CHART

circa 7,000 BC   Man is said to have come to Ireland from Scotland, crossing the North Channel, centre of many future migrations and emigrations. The first inhabitants of Ireland are called the LARNIANS, after excavations at Larne on the Antrim Coast in 1935.

circa 2000 BC   North Antrim is a great mine for the manufacture of flints and axes: they are exported all over the British Isles.

circa 700BC-1 AD   Celtic migrations or war bands from Europe establish kingdoms on the British Mainland; they suppress the pre-Celtic populations. GAELIC culture is born. In Ireland the last of the pre-Celtic kingdoms submit in Ulster - the kingdoms east of Lough Neagh.

circa 200 AD-400 AD   Irish invaders of Britain are called *Scotti* by the Romans, who flee Britain by 450 AD. The Kingdom of Dalriada, with coastal Dunseverick as its capital, expands into Scottish Argyll (Scottish Dalriada) and its islands.

circa 432 AD   Patrick is said to have been brought to present-day southern Antrim as a slave: he escapes, to return many years later to evangelize most of Ireland. Niall of the Nine Hostages raids Britain about 400 AD. Niall is legendary and is said to be High-King or Emperor (*Árd Rí*) of Ireland.

circa 500-850   Columba, a chieftain of western Ulster, expands the Gaelic Church into Scotland and Northern England. His missionaries, during and after his death, establish monasteries in Europe, and counsel to the great tribal German Emperor Charlemagne. NORSE INVASIONS, *circa* 795 AD. DECLINE OF GAELIC CHRISTIAN

CIVILIZATION.

circa 850-1169   Norse invasions divide Antrim Dalriada from Scottish Dalriada (Argyll). Antrim Dalriada takes her place alongside the O'Neill kingdom of Central and Western Ulster, and the other clans. Ulster continues the struggle with the southern clans of Ireland for All-Ireland rule. The Irish and Scots have visions of a Scots-Irish dual monarchy or empire, as the Normans invade England in 1066. NORMAN INVASION OF IRELAND 1169.

circa 1169-1300   The Normans only succeed in subduing the Antrim Coast and present-day County Down: they cannot establish a lasting hegemony in the rest of Ulster or in the rest of Ireland: their effective power is confined to the eastern seaboard, ruling from strongholds like Carrickfergus Castle, Dundrum Castle and Dublin Castle (in southern Ireland). The Norse are driven out of Ireland by the Irish and Normans, at a battle near Dublin in 1170. Scots Gallowglasses cross the North Channel to settle in Ulster, to help fight the Normans (1258). The Normans create the EARLDOM OF ULSTER in 1264. BEGINNING OF THE IRISH PARLIAMENT 1297.

circa 1315-1400   The Scots fear the Normans as well. Edward Bruce invades Ireland via Larne in south-east Antrim in another attempt by the Scots and Irish to establish a Gaelic dual monarchy. However famine and Scots cruelty alienate the Irish Gaels from the Scots Gaels, despite the fact that the *Scotti* of Antrim had given their name to Scotland after settling in Argyll, before the age of Saint Patrick. THE BLACK DEATH 1348 wipes out one third of Ireland's population.

circa 1400-1485 Decline of Norman power and dynastic war in England (the Wars of the Roses) gives Gaelic Ireland a chance of independence. The Ulster kingdoms persue a vigorously independent line, led by the O'Neills of Tyrone. The end of the Plantagenet Norman dynasty in England sees the English struggling for command in Ireland: English Common Law and Irish Gaelic Law conflict, as the English kings, like the Norman kings, expect the O'Neills and other Irish chiefs to hold their land from the Crown.

circa 1485-1588 PROTESTANT ideas reach Ulster. Henry VIII breaks with Rome and is made King and Head of the Church in England and Ireland.
Protestantism in England repulses the Spanish Armada in 1588. The Ulster chiefs treat the ship-wrecked Spaniards better than the southern clans. The rise and fall of the Catholic Shane O'Neill (1542-1567) in the reign of Henry VIII and Elizabeth I. He resists the imposition of English law, and by implication Protestantism in Ulster. He is assassinated at Cushendun in 1567.

circa 1588-1603 The rise and fall of Hugh O'Neill, nephew of Shane, and an English-educated Gaelic "king" of Ulster. He surrenders on 30 March 1603 after a protracted struggle with Elizabeth I.
EFFECTIVE END OF GAELIC POWER IN IRELAND. THE TRIUMPH OF ENGLISH LAW.

circa 1603-1607 The defeated Gaelic earls are restored, but they take fright, and flee to Europe when they are indicted on conspiracy charges. O'Neill and O'Donnell take ship from Rathmullen: THE FLIGHT OF THE EARLS, 1607.

circa 1607-1628 The plantation of Ulster is projected.

circa 1628-1641 150,000 Lowland Scots and 20,000 Englishmen "plant" Ulster. Eventually the Catholics only possess 500,000 acres out of 4,000,000 acres. 12·5 percent of Ulster was chosen by the Crown for plantation; but Chichester, the Lord Deputy of Ireland, recommended only 6·5 percent should be taken, leaving the Catholics in possession of most of the land.

circa 1641-1642 The Catholics rebel in Ulster, led by Owen Roe O'Neill, a relative of Shane and Hugh. It is said that there were great massacres carried out by both Protestants and Catholics. Divisions amongst Protestants leads to the establishment of THE PRESBYTERIAN CHURCH IN IRELAND on 10 June 1642.

circa 1642-1649 The Monarchy is overthrown in England because of financial and religious reasons; but Ulster Protestants (Presbyterians and Anglicans) do not support Oliver Cromwell, the fanatical Puritan. Realizing Cromwell is an enemy to Monarchy, the Protestants "unite" with the Catholics in order to defeat the political aspects of English Puritanism. The Catholic Confederacy of Anglicans, Presbyterians and Old English Catholics, is defeated after the fierce massacres of Drogheda and Wexford.

circa 1652-1690 Death of Cromwell in 1658. The defeat of Gaelic Ireland means that the Catholic Church in the British Isles makes its last stand in Ireland under the deposed Catholic King James II, once the Monarchy has been restored for a generation. Protestants and Catholics are clearly divided, religiously as always, and now politically.

SIEGE OF LONDONDERRY 1689. BATTLE OF THE BOYNE 1690.

circa 1700-1707 Scotland and England are united, along with Ireland, in a British Isles Monarchy, after the religious wars of the seventeenth century. Before 1707 the Monarchy viewed itself as purely English: the British Empire overseas was starting to rise. Penal laws against Roman Catholics and Protestant Dissenters entrench the Established Church's position. Ulster Protestants identify with the BRITISH MONARCHY; Roman Catholics are opposed to it on religious grounds.

GLOSSARY

The terms "Northern Ireland" and "Ulster" for the modern mind have led to much political debate. This book covers the period Before Christ to 1700 when a variety of terms were used, but when political bitterness, mixed with religious hatred, did not predominate in the Protestant-Catholic context for most of the time. ULAID is the ancient historical term, meaning "Ulster"; but the chieftains and peasants of Ulaid were not conscious that they were or should be a united kingdom or province. Ulaid therefore was a cultural term for a tribal confederacy, just as Ulster is a cultural term today used to cover up (or accept) the division of Ulster, being the Nine Counties of Antrim, Down, Londonderry, Fermanagh, Tyrone, Armagh, Cavan, Monaghan and Donegal. The ancient period (second century - fifth century) sees Ulaid divided into the following kingdoms:-

Dalriada	North Antrim and Scottish Argyll
Dál nAraidi	South Antrim and West Down.
Dál Fiatach	East County Down
Kingdom of Aileach (Northern Kingdom)	The Lands lying between the River Bann and the River Foyle and Upper and Lower Lough Erne.
Inishowen	The peninsula between Lough Foyle and Lough Swilly.
Tirconnell	Present-day County Donegal, but excluding Inishowen (see above).
Kingdom of Oriel	The lands lying between the River Blackwater, the Lower Bann and the Lower Erne.
Brefni	A kingdom straddling the present-day border of Northern Ireland and Eire.

By the time of Saint Patrick (*circa* 432 AD) Dalriada, Dál nAraidi and Dál Fiatach had become united, under Gaelic attack, into the Kingdom of Ulidia, but Ulidia was eventually submerged. The "capital" of Ulaid was *Emain Macha*, a hill fortress near present-day Armagh.

The term "Ulster" came into use in Norman times. The Normans claimed a theoretical suzereignty over all the above kingdoms or clanships; but effective authority was only over Inishowen (see above), Northern Aileach(see above), and Antrim and Down. This was the Norman EARLDOM OF ULSTER. Our knowledge of early Ulster is mainly from sources like the *Annals of Ulster*, written down from oral traditions in early Christian times. These early myths and legends contain many facts. The kingdoms of Ulster were part of the general GAELIC TRIBAL CONFEDERACY or HIGH-KINGSHIP. The head of this was the *Árd Rí*: like the *Inca* in Inca Civilization, he was the head of an illiterate civilization, until the introduction of Christianity. Ulster kings often became the *Árd Rí* or fought over the High-Kingship.

GENERAL

CELTS: A general term embracing many European tribal kingdoms. They came to the British Isles about 700 BC, conquered Ireland and became known as the GOIDELS or GAELS. They may also have come via the Celtic Sea, entering Ireland from the south.

DRUIDS: The religious leaders of the Celts.

ENGLISH: The people who evolved out of Norman England and who started to speak English by the fifteenth century. They brought Scotland and Ireland within the British Isles system.

GAELS: The Celts who settled in Ireland and Scotland, having their own version of Gaelic, in turn evolving into different forms. The Celts of Wales and Brittany spoke a different form of Gaelic.

IRISH: The language and people who evolved out of Gaelic Civilization.

LARNIANS: The pre-Celtic and original inhabitants of Ireland, thought to have come from Scotland. Named after the town of Larne in County Antrim where excavations were made in 1935. After them came the MEGALITH BUILDERS.

NORMANS: Continental invaders of Viking origin who invaded the British Isles, conquered England (1066) and reduced Gaelic Ireland (1169) and contained Gaelic Scotland.

SCOTS: The people who evolved out of general Gaelic Civilization, who had always an accepted foothold in Ireland. European Celts were converted to CHRISTIANITY (*circa* fifth century or before).

VIKINGS: The Norse from Norway and the Danes from Denmark, who established kingdoms along the Irish Coast.

POPULATION, KINGDOMS AND CLANS

POPULATION OF IRELAND (a *rough* guide):-

AD	
1 - 800	less than 500,000
800 - 1000	1,000,000
1000 - 1400	1,000,000
1400 - 1600	600,000 - 800,000
1600 - 1700	800,000 - 1,200,000

IRISH KINGDOMS

The main kingdoms by the Middle Ages, probably based upon the pre-Celtic population, were:-

ULIDIA   (north-east Ireland)

NORTHERN   (north-west Ireland)
ORIEL   (north-central Ireland)
LEINSTER   (south-east Ireland)
MEATH   (mid-central Ireland)
MUNSTER   (south-west Ireland)
CONNAUGHT   (mid-west Ireland)

The Norse were driven out of Ireland by the Middle Ages; their kingdoms and towns were:-
NORSE KINGDOM OF DUBLIN   (sixty miles covering the mid-central eastern littoral)
NORSE CITY OF WEXFORD   (and its environs)
NORSE CITY OF WATERFORD   "
NORSE CITY OF CORK   "
NORSE CITY OF LIMERICK   "

CLANS

By 1500 the Gaelic clans in Ulster, under pressure from England, emerged into the following:-

MacDonnell	Glens of South Antrim
MacQuillan	"the Route" of North Antrim
O'Neill	Present-day Counties Londonderry, Tyrone and Armagh, and part of West Antrim.
Magennis	The Iveagh of Western County Down
O'Doherty	Inishowen (see above).
MacSweeny	Western littoral of Donegal
O'Donnell	Most of Donegal.
Maguire	Lower Lough Erne.
O'Hanlon	Armagh City and district
O'Ruairc	West Brefni (see above).
O'Reilly	East Brefni (see above).
MacMahon	South Armagh

(The most celebrated of these clans, challenging the authority of England, were the O'Neills and the O'Donnells).

THE TERM ULSTER, therefore, did not come into existence until the thirteenth century, after which the term "Province of Ulster" was used by England. As Gaelic power declined , four Irish provinces emerged under British power by 1700:-

LEINSTER   (south-east Ireland, capital Dublin).
MUNSTER   (south-west Ireland, capital Cork).
CONNAUGHT   (mid-central western Ireland, capital Galway).
and ULSTER   (capital Londonderry; later Belfast).

PRONUNCIATION OF IRISH NAMES AND TERMS

	Pronounced
Aileach	*Al-yuch*
Árd Rí	*Aurd-Ree*
Dalriada	*Dal-ree-ada*
Druim Cett	*Drum Kat*
Emain Macha	*Emmun Macha*
Eoghanacht	*Owen-acht*
Feis	*Fesh*
Fir Bolg	*Fir Bollug*
Iveagh	*Ivy*
Kavanagh	*Kav-an-a*
Mogh Nuadat	*Moe-Nooadat*
Murchertach	*Mur-Kertach*
Murrough	*Murr-uch*
Niall	*Nee-al*
O Ruairc	*O Roo-irk*
Shane	*Shaan (Irish Seán)*
Tír Eoghain	*Teer Owen*
Tuath	*Tooath*
Tyrconnell	*Tirr-connell*
Uí Néill	*Ee Nayl*

FOREWORD

The English arrived late in Ireland, and even later in Ulster. They had not become fully English until the strain of the Norman invasions had died out by the fifteenth century. Gaelic Civilization itself was preceded by many centuries of primitive culture - in the north of Ireland it is noted for the remains of the megalith tomb builders.

An historical north/south conflict has always existed in Ireland, that a series of invasions - the Celts from Europe, the Vikings from Scandinavia, the Normans from France via England, and the English themselves - helped to accentuate. The religious and political conflicts of sixteenth and seventeenth-century England helped to embitter relations between the English and Irish, and between Ulster and the south of Ireland, as they had never been embittered before.

Invasions had not all been from outside Ireland: the *Scotti* raiders of Ulster gave their name to Scotland and were a real menace to the declining Roman Empire in Britain during the third to fifth centuries: the Irish colonized the western coast of Britain at a time when the Catholic Church was expanding from Europe. Saint Patrick came to Ireland - many people believe to Ulster - about 432 AD, an invasion of a different kind.

It is tempting to ask the question: have all the invasions stopped? Will history throw up yet another wave of invasions, which she has never failed to do in the past, another people who might conquer England, or a different kind of Englishman, to again complicate the north/south of Ireland conflict? Gaelic and English Law would then be put firmly in the history books.

The world of Saint Patrick is about forty-four generations displaced from the Troubles of the twentieth century. The world of the Protestant Plantation, starting in 1607, is only twelve generations displaced: the past may be closer than is imagined: both northern and southern Irishmen have believed this for centuries, and the problems of Ireland appear to have confirmed this.

Before and during the expansion of the Gaelic Church, followed by the Viking and Norman invasions, we are dealing with an Ulster (Ulaid) that had taken on no definite form. It had links with Scotland from the Stone Age, links which were continued at the time of Saint Patrick; these were continued throughout the Middle Ages, to the present day, sometimes for good sometimes for bad.

It has often been forgotton that at one time both Scots and Irish were Gaels, of which they were politically very conscious in the early Middle Ages. It is part of the story of Ulster - and an intrinsic part of Irish history - to understand this great rupture between Scots and Irish. Taking place during the expansion of the English Monarchy, let us see the role the Ulster Scots played.

MICHAEL SHEANE - *September 1980*

Part One

SAINTS AND
SCHOLARS

A CATHOLIC MONARCHY

During the sixteenth century, the Scottish earls were crossing the North Channel to settle in the green glens and sweeping bays of north-east Ulster. The English Monarchy ruled uncertainly under the Tudors: the Scottish earls, Catholics themselves, had no idea that Henry VIII would break with tradition and with Catholicism by 1531. Ireland had always held true to its own version of the Faith: like the French Roman Catholic Church of the eighteenth century, the Irish Catholic Church preferred to hover on the periphery of Rome, rather than to endorse its international outlook. Since the Middle Ages, the Popes had strove to wield Christendom into a unified civilization, to control the rising national monarchies and their churches. The Irish Catholic Church looked back to Saint Patrick and Saint Columba. Its independence of Rome ceased to exist by 1000 AD. The See of Armagh rose to be its centre and the green fields of Antrim were said to be its nuturing ground. When Ireland was invaded by England in 1169, at the invitation of its warring chieftains, the Irish Church was brought into even greater conformity with the Papacy.

When the Tudor dynasty succeeded to power in England in 1485, Ireland was ruled by the Anglo-Irish earls of Kildare; the Kildares attempted to rule parts of Ulster from the English "Pale" area centred around Dublin, the seat of administration. The "cold north" became the stronghold of the Gaelic way of life. English colonizers pushed further and further into the Irish heart land. Gaelic culture was surviving, but it lived in a doomed world. For the English of the late sixteenth century, as the spectre of colonialism arose, the New World started on the beaches of Cornwall and Devon: boat load after boat load of adventurers

1

reached the south of Ireland, amongst them the young Sir Walter Raleigh. Ireland was to be treated no differently than Virginia in America: unlike the American colonies its resources were relatively restricted. The Gaelic culture was a tired one: gone were the days of Saint Patrick when Ireland arose to be one of the foremost ecclesiastical centres in Europe and when Irish monks counselled to the great German Emperor Charlemagne in the ninth century. The Gaels never existed for long under unity of a local prince or emperor. Internecine warfare was the rule, and Ireland's weakness became England's opportunity: the Tudors demanded imperial splendour for their Crown, and like the Normans, they proceeded to make themselves "Lords of Ireland"; but it was not until 1541 - after Henry VIII's break with Rome in 1531 - and when the forces of anti-Protestantism had gathered strength, that they made themselves Kings of the country. Between the end of the Norman Age and the coming of the Welsh Tudors, Ireland enjoyed a measure of local independence under its Anglo-Norman earls: in the south the Earl of Kildare had ignored England's laws of intermarriage with the Irish; his own family were linked in marriage with the O'Neills, the greatest warring lords of Ulster. Intermarriage with the Irish had earned many of the Anglo-Irish the title of "degenerate English". To the *nova riche* Tudors, surviving in the international uncertainty of the Reformation world, these "degenerate English" were English rulers that had colonized Ireland, but had fallen foul of local habits. The Tudor Age saw the tightening grip of England on her disintegrating Irish realm. Though Ireland lived on the fringe of civilized Europe, her trading contacts were extensive: Irish ships could be seen in the Baltic and Irish traders at the great fairs of Brabant; she exported to Spain and Italy. Hides and fish(salmon, hake and herring), wool, linen cloth, the skins of otters, squirrels, sheep and kids were the products of what England regarded as a pioneering land. Outside of the English-ruled areas or "pales" lived and hunted and fought, the native Irish, dark-eyed and emotionally Gaelic, resentful of the invading master. The Irish

2

started to remember the greatness of the Gaelic Heroic Age; but they were now an older race - older than the warriors that had put faith in Saint Patrick and had spread the Catholic Church, an individual Gaelic one, to many parts of the British Isles and Europe by 800 AD.

A long revolution started as the Middle Ages closed in Europe, but which lingered on in Ireland until the seventeenth century. The Universal Civilization of the Popes was passing away; the Papacy's temporal power was being diminished; periphery countries like Ireland came under colonial assault by expanding national monarchies. In Ulster, where the lords of the north could defend themselves in the mountains of Tyrone and in the wastelands of Donegal, the Gaels were to make a final stand. The lords of the north, like American Sitting Bulls, confronted an English Civilization that was as alien to them as a cannon was to a bow and arrow. The great lakes of Ulster like Upper and Lower Lough Erne, surrounded by forests, and the broad expanse of Lough Neagh, the greatest inland lake in the British Isles, were for the English the trapping grounds of animal and Irishman; and the graveyard of many Englishmen. The Scottish coast lay only twelve miles from Northern Antrim. For the Gaelic Irishman, used to the Scots coming and going across the North Channel since before Christ, the Scot was of a similar race, and until Henry VIII's break with Rome, of the same Catholic faith. Scots Catholics came from the Highlands and Islands to Catholic Ulster, to eventually head such clans as the great MacDonnells of the Glens of Antrim. Before the time of Robert Bruce (1315), a Scots King that envisaged a Scots-Irish dual monarchy, there had been dreams of a unified Gaelic nation: a Gaelic nation might stand against the over mighty arrogance of the Anglo-Saxons. The Anglo-Saxons, of German origin, interbred with their Norman conquerors after 1066, driving the remaining Gaelic communities westwards and imposing more Continental systems. For the Gaels, the English were a very mixed nation; the English rested content under the Norman system; they did not buckle under the

3

conqueror, but assimilated him.

At the close of the Middle Ages, Wales and Ireland, and then Scotland, disintegrated in front of the expanding Catholic Monarchy of England, possessed by the Normans. England proceeded, with the blessing of Pope Adrian IV in 1155, to establish as an Irish Lordship. Suspicion, then hate of England, forced the Scots Catholics in Ulster and Irish Catholics together in an alliance that had its roots in centuries of intercourse between the coasts and headlands: the lands bordering the North Channel (of both Scotland and Ireland) represented a thalassocracy of flimsy ships sailing on the cold sun-lit seas, viewing the highlands and islands and glens. By the fifteenth century, one of the Earls of Antrim had become the Lord of the Isles, as this Medieval thalassocracy has been styled. Like the Greeks of Ancient History, the Scots-Irish of north-eastern Ulster, and Argyll in Scotland, could cry *Thàlassa! Thalassa!* The Sea! The Sea! The sea was a symbol of freedom in this mysterious Gaelic and Catholic world, full of crimson sunsets and cautious people. The Norman invader, in his robust armour, European methods of warfare, and impregnable defence, was far in advance of the Gaels. The Gaels had indefinable attractions: intermarriage and interbreeding became the rule. The Gael was a man dressed in fur and linen, carrying a leather shield and a bow and arrow, speaking a different language and observing different laws. Only in Ulster, as Gaelic Civilization disintegrated in the south of Ireland were the Gaels able to make a last stand.

English invasions of the south of Ireland, the destruction of the Kingdom of Munster in the south west by the end of the sixteenth century, further demarcated the south of Ireland from the Scots-Irish north: this had lingered on, even in Catholic circles to the present day. Scots warriors, the Gallowglasses, had from the early Middle Ages, crossed from the Scots Isles to hack out Irish Kingdoms; whilst during the fifth century, in the age of Saint Patrick, the men of Antrim had used the North Channel to invade Argyll and its surrounding islands, to establish the Kingdom of

4

Dalriada. "Dalriada" meant Antrim: its capital, during the ascendancy of Antrim Dalriada, was Dunseverick, near Benbane Head and the Giant's Causeway, on the stormy coast of Northern Antrim. Dunseverick lay at the end of the great north-south highway.

The first Tudor King of England, Henry VII (1485-1509) had an eye for economy: he preferred to rule Ireland through great lords like the Kildares. Ulster was out of Henry VII's and Kildare's reach. Henry VII's son, Henry VIII (1509-1547) continued the policy of hating the over mighty subject in England, but like his father he could not apply it to Ireland. Gaels and English were not to be kept separate, and there was to be no distinction between Anglo-Irish and Gaelic earls. The policy was perhaps aimed to woo the lords of the north, especially the O'Neills of central Ulster. The law of hereditary succession, the backbone of English aristocratic law, conflicted with the Gaelic law of Tanistry: the native custom was to select any of the near relatives of a dead chieftain: this often gave rise to endless feuds, and prevented Ireland from becoming a united national state like England. The Gaelic peasants regarded themselves as owning the land: they did not hold the land, as in England, from a feudal overlord. For a while English principles were accepted: the chieftains saw hereditary succession as a means to preserve their declining powers, as England encroached upon their domains; the peasants would not acquiesce when the chieftains selected their eldest sons. Moreover when Henry VIII broke with Rome in 1531 the native chieftains were eventually bound to accept the King as head of the Church of England and to reject the Pope's version of the Catholic faith, a policy that the ordinary Irish soon loathed. Henry VIII's new church was not as yet revolutionary in doctrine, and so Catholicism as traditionally practised, remained for a short time intact. As in England, the bait of monastic land was offered to create vested interests that would establish his revolution. But the Reformation in Ireland was not so bloody as in England. The Catholic Church, said Martin Luther, Europe's first Protestant, had sunk into material corruption and doctrinal error. The Tudors became Protestant Defenders of the Faith ruling Gaelic Catholics in Ireland.

THE REFORMATION

The religious and political struggles of the Reformation were to rend seventeenth-century Ulster apart: the struggles have lived on into the twentieth century, and they took official root when the Dublin Parliament had to confer the title of "King of Ireland" on the Protestant Henry VIII in 1541. The Lordship of Ireland had been granted to the Norman Kings of England by Pope Adrian IV in 1155, the only Englishman to have been Pope. Protestant rule in Ireland was only apparent; in practice the Papacy still appointed bishops to Irish sees, especially in Ulster, where the important bishoprics of Raphoe, Derry and Armagh were firmly within the Papal grasp; whilst in 1539, in the Munster province of south-west Ireland, two archbishops and eight bishops accepted Henry VIII as "Supreme Head". Henry however would not abandon his policy of diplomacy in Ireland, for in view of England's uncertain international position, his policy still had to be one of caution. There were also great military difficulties facing a complete Irish takeover: the Scots and Irish of the North viewed it in a friendly light that the Kingdom of Scotland should invade England, and the Irish chieftains kept large retinues. Meanwhile the destruction of revered images and relics went on. The monasteries were despoiled. The forces of Rome would soon be launched against Protestant England from Spain and France; but England had learnt from experience that foreign invasion of Ireland was always difficult and seldom supported for long by the Irish. Opposition in England to the newly-established Anglican Church, which accepted Catholicism in principle until the death of Henry VIII in 1547, meant attention on domestic affairs. The break with Rome, however, inevitably meant the break with Catholicism as it had been practised for centuries; the forces of

6

outright Protestantism, and the forces of Puritanism - and of Presbyterianism - would rear their heads, condemning the traditions of the Latin and Greek Church fathers, and rejecting the authority of bishops, Roman or Anglican. Revolution at the top was to be followed by upheaval and total Reformation at the bottom. Ulster was then firmly Catholic like the rest of Ireland, perhaps more Catholic because of its independent position; more than the other Irish kingdoms, its natives were more alien to English Common Law, particularly to the principle of hereditary succession. But Henry VIII, mentally disturbed in his old age, and frustrated with his many wives, did not regard himself as "a Protestant": in England he hanged Catholics as traitors and Protestants as heretics.

It seemed as if the Reformation would run a relatively peaceful course in Ireland. The Parliament of 1541 was well attended by ecclesiastics, nobles, gentry and the new wealthy middle classes; Irish chiefs were present. The bill conferring the Kingship of Ireland upon Henry VIII was read in Irish and the title was publicly proclaimed in Saint Patrick's Cathedral after a solemn mass song by the Anglican Archbishop of Dublin. Henry, as "Supreme Head of the Church and Clergy of England", revered the ancient Catholic nature of the Faith, and condemned its Roman variation - a variation or corruption that the Church of England started to claim had taken place after the end of Primitive Christianity in about 300 AD: the fourth-century Roman Emperor Constantine, by making Christianity the state religion, is said to have brought a lot of worldliness and sophistication into the Church. The Church of Rome, according to the German revolutionary Martin Luther (whom Henry VIII had blasted in 1521, later receiving the title of *Fedei Defensor* from the Pope) had acquired onto itself such deviations as the Doctrine of Papal Primacy, Indulgences and the Cult of the Virgin Mary. The Church of Rome replied that although the official body of the Church was wanting much, and also weighed down by worldly corruption, it would not prevent it, after vigorous reformation

7

from within, from taking on a new lease of Christian life. Anglicans, who now started to undermine traditional doctrines like Transubstantiation,*did not trust the Church of Rome. Henry VIII's matrimonial difficulties, the growing nationalism of the English Monarchy, and the independent economy of England, were used to engineer the break with Rome. Henry VIII only formalized a political position that in practice had already existed *vis-à-vis* the Church in England; in Europe, national monarchs had already considerable influence over the Catholic Church in their own countries. For a while Ireland acquiesced in the Reformation. "The usurped authority of the bishop of Rome" was renounced by the Scots-Irish of Antrim and purely Irish of Kerry alike; and the peasant rested content that no great change in ritual (what Protestants would later regard as superstition) had been made. But bread and butter issues, often inflaming religious passions, entered this Reformation. The Law of Hereditary Succession, accepted for a while by the Gaelic earls, deprived the peasant of ownership of the land; the land that had been held in trust by the chiefs, now accepting English titles. Under English feudal law the peasant did not own his own plot. Henry VIII hoped that Primogeniture, whereby property fell to the eldest son, would end the chronic local feuds: these typified not only Ulster, but the rest of Ireland. An Englishman, writing at the time, said of the Irish petty states or *tuatha,* that:-

"There be more than sixty countries, called regions, in Ireland, inhabited with the king's Irish enemies ... where reigneth more than sixty captains ... that liveth by the sword and obeyth to no temporal person, but only to himself that is strong: and every of the said captains maketh war and peace for himself, and holdeth by the sword, and hath imperial jurisdiction within his room, and obeyeth to no other person, English or Irish, except

---

* The doctrine that states that the Bread and the Wine in the Mass are trully, substantially and wholly the Body and the Blood of Jesus Christ. Anglicans eventually adopted the Doctrine of Holy Communion, making the bread and the wine symbols of Christ's blood. Anti-Episcopalians, like the Presbyterians, reject the Anglican ceremony surrounding Holy Communion.

only to such persons as may subdue him by the sword ... Also, there is more than thirty great captains of the English noble folk, that followeth the same Irish order ... and every of them maketh war and peace for himself, without licence of the king, or of any other temporal person, save of him that is strongest, and of such as may subdue them by the sword."

Irish society was geared to war and local dispute, whilst English kingship in England had achieved, and represented in Ireland, law and order, one war lord that in England had subdued all the others, and who was now usurping the authority of the Pope. Henry VIII entrusted the task of re-organizing Ireland to Sir Anthony St Leger: he ruled between 1540-1548. He persuaded the strong Gaelic chieftains like O'Neill of Tyrone in central Ulster, to surrender their Gaelic titles and receive them back under English names: this policy of "Surrender and Re-grant" dated back to the Normans. However the English Monarchy became more Protestant under the boy King Edward VI (1547-1553), and the internecine nature of Irish society persisted inspite of the new imposed English system.

Attempts to re-organize Ireland in Henry VIII's reign (1509-1547) had led to the invasion of the English Pale area, centred round Dublin, by the great O'Neill of Ulster, to whom Ireland increasingly looked for leadership. A temporary peace followed. Frequent changes of English administration, and the intrigues of the Earls of Desmond in south-west Ireland to ally with the King of France in 1523, and with the Emperor Charles V in 1528, were to add thunder and lightning to the piling clouds banking up from a hostile and Catholic Europe. It had been the task of the Earls of Kildare to counteract anti-English influences. As local Anglo-Irish chieftains, the Kildares had not only political ambitions in Ireland, but private ambitions for their family. Henry VII's reign (1485-1509) was supposed to have seen the end of the feudal influence of the House of Kildare: the economy and throne-minded Henry VII preferred a system of direct administration from England. This was to prove more costly, especially in military terms. The re-conquest of Ireland after the Norman period (1169-1399) meant the final, and most bloody, challenge to the Gaelic world.

The extension of the power of the Kildare family had of course excluded most of Ulster; the earl's expeditions were stopped short at County Down, whilst he was content to intermarry with central Ulster clans like the O'Neills and western clans like the Burkes and the O'Donnells. The Tudors looked uncannily at the power of Kildare, since the Kildares had supported the Yorkists during the Wars of the Roses. Kildare had the Yorkist Lambert Simnel crowned in Christ Church, Dublin, on 24 May 1487 as a rival to Henry VII. The Irish Parliament, sitting at Drogheda, was subdued by Sir Edward Poynings in 1494. Poyning's Law stated that all bills introduced into the Irish Parliament must first have the consent of the English Privy Council and the Crown. Direct administration still proved difficult,and the tendency was always to fall back upon local magnates; so the traditional power of the magnates, as held since Norman times, enjoyed an artificial life up to the reign of Henry VIII. But an effective local magnate meant an ineffective English King. The more effective local power became in Ireland, especially in Ulster, the more England conspired at its overthrow. The ideal was never achieved of gaining a submissive local magnate or power that would sincerely acknowledge English authority; whilst local leaders never arose that were content to wield local power, without making pretensions to Irish national influence. It appeared that there were basic political antipathies between the two islands, and between local powers in Ireland. Local power worked not only for the destruction of despotic central authority, but against all-Ireland central rule, either under Englishman or Gael. A resurgent Roman Church was ineffective as yet: the Jesuit missionaries who arrived in Ulster in 1542 with letters from the Pope and from Ignatius Loyola, founder of the Order, received a hostile welcome; they could conveniently escape over the North Channel and into Catholic Scotland, which would soon fall under the influence of John Knox and Calvinism. However the friars still preached against the Tudor Monarchy and exhorted the Gaelic peasants to work for the restoration of Papal authority. The Church of Rome was forced to rely on the people and the people started to get to know "Holy Mother Church". Radical changes in doctrine were to keep the Reformation alive in the British Isles for Protestants; when these changes came in the reign of Edward VI (1547-1543), a gulp opened between the Gaelic peasants and the new Protestant authorities and their supporters. An édition of the English Book of Common Prayer of 1549 was printed in Dublin, the first book to be printed in Ireland. Its Protestantism however was rejected by the Irish Anglican bishops: they would prefer a return to Papal authority, rather than deny the Mass and reject ancient traditions. George Dowdall, Archbishop of Armagh, went into exile rather than accept the Book of Common Prayer, exclaiming that "he would never be a bishop where the holy mass was abolished". He reconciled himself with the Papacy, and was reappointed as rebel Archbishop of the see. The reign of Bloody Mary (1553-1558) re-established the primacy of the Pope, but still the political and cultural gulp yawned between Ireland and England: despite Mary's return to Catholicism, O'Neill and O'Donnell in Ulster, who had been willing to risk matters with Henry VIII, made alliances with Henry VII of France, head of the Catholic League in Europe, to safeguard their political independence against Catholic England.

The return of Roman Catholicism under Bloody Mary (Mary I), saw English rule tighten its grip upon Ireland as the policy of plantation in the easier subdued south began. The Ulster earls, Catholic or "Protestant" were intent upon keeping English power back, as was traditional. The followers of the MacDonnells of the Western Isles of Scotland, who had gained a grip upon North Antrim, became known as the "Redshanks" of the Glens. They were Scots Catholics, hiring themselves out to the other Gaelic chiefs. Meanwhile the Desmonds were gathering forces in south-west Ireland. The English attempted to penetrate the Gap of the

11

North between Dundalk and Newry: the Gap of the North guarded the warring kingdoms of Ulster from the south. In 1556 the English managed, like the Normans before them, to penetrate to the Lagan Valley, and to fight their way to the southern shores of the Antrim Coast. Mary I did not last long: the return of Protestantism under Elizabeth I (1558-1603) flung all of Ireland into conflagration. Warring lord after warring lord challenged the Protestant English mistress and "harlot" Queen that tried to ape the role of Saint Peter, double infamy and double blasphemy in itself. The events previous to the five Tudor monarchs had done much to set the Reformation scene; they also laid the foundations of the modern Scottish link in north-east Ulster, with the Plantation of Ulster after the death of Elizabeth I in 1603.

THALASSOCRACY OF THE NORTH

The Scots influence in Ulster had become considerable from the thirteenth century. The fighting gallowglasses (*gall-oglaigh* or foriegn soldiers) from the Outer Hebrides, were enlisted by the Irish chieftains to combat the encroaching power of the Normans, who had invaded Ireland in 1169. Carrickfergus Castle, on the banks of Belfast Lough, conveniently situated opposite Chester in Northern England, the chief port to Ireland, was the Norman's main base in Ulster. The great Ulster clans, like the O'Neills, hired the gallowglasses, who came over the North Channel, to keep the clever Normans at bay. Ulster kept true to her independent role of defending herself longer than the other kingships: she was geographically isolated behind a barrier of lakes and mountains, that could only be breached at the Moyry Pass (Gap of the North) and at the fords of Erne. From an invaders point of view her raw materials and agricultural potential were less than the rest of Ireland: there was more gold in the Wicklow Mountains than in the Antrim Hills. Like the barbaric Germans of the third and fourth century Roman Empire, the Ulster lords were an especial symbol of fear. Most of the Norman towns were situated on the eastern coast of central and southern Ireland. Norman Ireland like the Ireland of the Protestant Tudors, was restricted in effect to "the Pale" area around Dublin. The Irish were slow absorbers of the Normans; whilst in Ulster the process of intermarriage and interplay between the Irish and Scots was considerable. As the fighting gallowglasses drove their way with their huge axes into southern Ireland against the Normans, isolated colonies of Scots grew up, but died out in later centuries. Only in the north of Ireland, in the lands bordering the Antrim Coast and in the northern Donegal region did the Scots-Irish form a community apart that had lasting potential. The Scots were the only accepted settlers in Ireland: in the far west of Ulster, in Tyrconnell, the great O'Donnell clan presented a formidable obstacle to Norman and English rule. However the Normans, and Scots, surrounded by the Gaelic Irish, were always conscious that they had come into possession of land that was not theirs; but still they became "more Irish than the Irish themselves". They sought to justify their long-term future in Ireland. This was easier to achieve on the northern coast of Ireland: here the constant coming and going had taken place between the Highlands and Western Isles of Scotland from Stone Age times. The North Channel, as a key route of communication, like the ancient thalassocracies of Greece, became a vital centre of this northern Irish/western Scottish culture. As centuries elapsed it became alien to purely Gaelic Ireland, developing a life style of its own, leaving its impress on Ulster. Scotland itself was uniting as a rival national monarchy, to threaten England, at the close of the Middle Ages.

The sixteenth century in Europe was an age of great westward migrations. England looked west, into Ireland, and to the New World. She was a maritime power like Spain and Portugal. Ireland had a population of about one million, and like native American culture, there was no united central power or advanced technology that might repulse the conqueror. Richard Hakluyt, the great promotor of travel and colonization, claimed that

English expansion into Ireland was caused by England's expanding population: "we are grown more populous than heretofore", and that "people can hardly live one by another, nay rather they are ready to eat up one another". Technologically backward countries like Ireland, America and the overseas colonial world generally, offered irresistible opportunities. But the Spanish, famed for their greed of gold in South America, could see the drawbacks of emigration as well as its attractions: it was the general policy to send out from England, Spain and Portugal men who hated work at home or men who wanted to get rich quick and who could deal with native populations with a minimum of conscience. The Scots migrations into Ulster in the sixteenth, and particulary the seventeenth centuries, was an overspill. Migrations had also been going on from Antrim Dalriada from the second half of the fifth century into Argyll, but history leaves us uncertain of the real character of these early migrations. The impression has often been created that Ulster is a cultural continuation of the west of Scotland: but during the Dalriada thalassocracy it was the west of Scotland that came under the hand of Ulaid and its fierce warriors, armed with Christianity. The Island of Iona, off the coast of Argyll, became a famed ecclesiastical centre by the end of the sixth century, from which missionaries went to France and Italy and to the court of the great German Emperor Charlemagne.

It has sometimes been pointed out that the later migrations from the west of Scotland in the seventeenth century, which established the Protestant Plantation of Ulster, could have been descendants of the early migrations from Antrim Dalriada. At the time of the *Dál Riada* sept there was no conception of an Irish or Scottish nation. Dalriada represented a sea kingdom of islands and coast lands and a cultural sphere. Certainly there could have been no sense of geographical unity between Scotland and Ireland outside of Dalriada, as there was likewise no sense of British Isles unity in England. Dalriada lasted in some form until the sixteenth century, ruled for a short time from Glenarm on the Antrim

Coast. By then the remaining island realms of Dalriada had become the Lordship of the Isles. The North Channel did not present an obstacle to communication; it was an essential ingredient in the north-east Ulster/western Isles culture. However the moorlands and plateaus that lay behind the Antrim Coast - and the Highlands of Scotland - presented the real obstacles to communications. Here dwelt the real natives, Irish and Scots. By the time of Henry VIII, England for the Scots and Irish, whether Protestant or Catholic, was the political enemy and expansionist force that threatened Gaelic life. During the reign of "Bloody Mary" (1553-1558), the Catholic Scots of Antrim were regarded as a real menace, and Parliament passed legislation to stop the further migration of Scots into Antrim: they threatened to take over all of Ulster; and perhaps eventually to dominate the whole of Ireland in competition with the migrating English. Thus the intercourse between the north coasts of Ulster with the west of Scotland had been going on since early Christian times, and before. The Scots did not suddenly appear in Ulster with the emigration policies of James I in 1607, after the great Gaelic earl of central Ulster, Hugh O'Neill, was overthrown. The North Channel cultural sphere had, and still has today, very clearly defined characteristics, if one studies the architecture, looks at the churches, and observes the many Scots characteristics of both Protestants and Catholics. Intercourse between the north of Ireland and the west of Scotland was longer during solely Catholic times (from the birth of Christ to 1600); whilst Scots Protestant Ulster, today one-third Catholic, has had a much smaller but a more explosive life.

Before the thirteenth century the "unity" of Antrim and Scottish Dalriada was a cultural and political phenomenon, with migrations coming more from the Ulster coast lands to the Highlands and Islands. The first great migrations back to Ulster comes with the gallowglasses. Internal feuds in Irish society generally gave these tall youthful warriors their chance: more than the Normans they found an acceptable role in Ireland. The

Lordship of the Isles lasted throughout the fifteenth century, resisting the hostility of the Scottish kings and enjoying the friendship of England. The Antrim Lordship stood separate from the Earls of Ulster, Norman based. When James IV of Scotland overran the more important Scottish part of the Lordship in 1499, the Antrim Scots were left with only a few of the lesser Scottish islands like Rathlin and Islay. The islanders fled to the Antrim Coast, to the stronghold of Glenarm. By 1550 James MacDonnell established himself in the Glens of Antrim, but an older branch of the race had been there since 1400. The Lords of the Glens had to deal with the encroaching Irish earls of Ulster, like the O'Neills, against whom at times ten-thousand Hebridean Scots, the "Redshanks", were employed. The Antrim Scots and the Scots of Donegal were faced by the power of ·Irish Gaelic arms, backed up by English forces, as Protestant England expanded throughout the island. By the sixteenth century England was determined to bring the independent power of both the Ulster Scots and the warring Irish into harness, and under a unified British Monarchy.

To the English soldier the gallowglasses were young men of huge physique, reared in the cold Hebridean north, Scots invaders of Ireland, that had come to hack out an Irish foothold, with all the terror of the Vikings, from whom they were descended. They were the cruel mercenaries of the Irish chiefs, that ever attempted like the American natives, to keep the Englishman out of his land. The Gaels wished to lead an independent and warlike life of their own. The gallowglasses aped European modes of warfare; they armed themselves with a shirt of mail, a skullcap of steel and a dagger; but most of all, and most deadly, was their mighty axe blade, six foot long with a knife-edge that could sever an Englishman's head at a blow and hack several of the English to pieces. The gallowglasses often returned to Scotland during the summer months across the North Channel. They sang their warlike songs, falling into romance on the deep waters, lit by the long evenings up till midnight. The "Redshanks" were the Highlanders, whilst the ordinary gallowglass could either be of

Scots or Irish origin. Depending upon the state of feud, they might return to Scotland over the winter, to dream over their log fires and to guard their own Highlands. The Lordship of the Isles was an admixture of Norse speakers, as in Shetland, and Gaelic speakers as in Lewis, Harris, the Uist and Barra. There was Skye, Rhum, Egg and Muck, Coll, Tiree, Colonsay, Islay and Jura, the great promontory of the Mull of Kintyre and the Isle of Arran, rearing like great rounded peaks out of the sea. The Lordship included Galloway, opposite Scots Antrim, and stretched south, embracing the Isle of Man. The Isle of Man was named after an Irish deity, Manannan and was an Irish dependency up till the earlier Viking age. One had to be an experienced sailor and know every shallow and rock to ply these stormy channels, that in hot windless nights enchanted the traveller. From the Isle of Lewis in the Hebrides ("Sudreyas" or Southern Isles to the northern-based Vikings) to the Isle of Man in the south, the Lordship of the Isles measured about three-hundred miles; in breadth from its associated lands in Donegal in the west of Ulster, to Galloway in the west of Scotland, it measured about one hundred and fifty miles. A traveller starting from Lough Swilly in Donegal, if he was not taking ship, had to negotiate the barrenness of Inishowen, either cross Lough Foyle by flimsy coracle (a skiff made of wickerwork and hides) or travel south, evading the dangerous clans, to reach Gaelic Derry on the banks of the Foyle estuary. The traveller would make his way up the Antrim Coast and its gale-torn headlands by uncertain routes, or risk it inland across the moorlands and clan-infested glens, living off the countryside as he went. Then at last he would reach the greener Glens of Antrim. If the traveller wished to cut short his journey, and if weather permitted, he could take boat at "the Route" Clanship in the area of the Giant's Causeway and be rowed to Rathlin Island, about five miles off the Antrim Coast. At Rathlin he could take bigger ship for the Mull of Kintyre, heading for Campbeltown or a secret cove; this would be a day's journey, but the Mull of Kintyre was always within sight of eye, looming like a large off-shore island. Perhaps somewhere in the south of the Antrim Lordship, perhaps at present-day Glenarm, or south at Olderfleet(Larne), one could brave the wider bottle neck of the North Channel, most certainly on a calm day. Here the sight of eye would not be so reliable; depending upon winds, the crossing to the Galloway coast could take up to two days. The journey from the north of the Lordship of the Isles to the south was safest under command of an experienced skipper. Ships were of modified Viking construction, up to one-hundred feet long, and generally under large square sails in this period of the late Middle Ages. Crew and traveller would wend their way past the islands, calling in where necessary for provisions, or to pick up passengers, or where weather threatened. At last the Isle of Man would be reached, perhaps after two weeks at sea.

WARRIOR LORDS

The Gallowglasses and the Normans were the descendants of the Vikings. The Vikings swept most of north-west Europe between the eighth and tenth centuries. Entering Ireland up the River Shannon, and sweeping down the Atlantic along the western and eastern coasts, the Norse from Norway and the Danes from Denmark, never succeeded in subduing the Scots or native Irish chieftains. They did however achieve a lasting foothold in the Lordship of the Isles, where they became the Gallowglasses. These Scandinavian pagans managed to gain a grip on the north of Ireland under their leader Turgesius. His long ships sailed up the River Bann into Lough Neagh. It is said that they appeared at Rathlin Island in the late eighth century. The Isle of Man was used as a strategic base for concerted attacks on the rest of the British Isles, under the second wave of invasions led by the Danes. The final invasions came in the tenth century. Both in the north and south the Irish fled to defend themselves in large round towers, *(cloiteachs)*, flung up over night. They fled in terror from these blond-haired barbarians that proceeded to destroy the rich Christian culture. Movements for Irish unity, to combat the Scandinavians, took root in west-central Ireland by the tenth century. For a while the chieftains succeeded in uniting around their *Árd Rí* or Emperor. At the Battle of Clontarf, near Dublin, in 1014, the *Árd Rí* Brian Boru drove out the Norse with great slaughter. From the time of the Scanidinavian invasions Gaelic Irishmen had learnt to deal with, and drive out, hostile settlers, seeking to impose their own language and life style. However Brian Boru had his skull cracked open by a Viking axe. At his death the Ardriship fell into warring feud amongst the competing jealous local kings. Brian Boru had been talked of as "Emperor of the Scots"; but comtemporary Irishmen, to whom this mostly referred, and some of whom had fought by the side of the Norse, with Ulster out of it, regarded this *Árd Rí* from the south as a usurper of a traditional title: this had descended from Niall of the Nine Hostages, the famous fourth century *Árd Rí* and Emperor: at this time the Irish were known as *Scotti* or raiders by the mainland Romano-British.

In the fourth and fifth centuries, with the Romans fleeing back to Europe to defend the Empire against barbarians from the east of Europe, barbarians from Ulster were attacking the British mainland: from Antrim Dalriada into Argyll to establish Scottish Dalriada and the Island Kingdoms; here they became known as the Scots; and from the south of Ireland into Wales and the Lake District, establishing temporary lordships in the decaying Roman world. It was on one of the many raiding expeditions made by Niall of the Nine Hostages, perhaps in 389 AD, that the Goidels are said to have brought back to the Slemish region of present-day County Antrim a slave called Succat: history remembers Succat as Saint Patrick. It is said that he was already Christian when he was captured. He was destined to alter the whole course of Irish history. Like other Christian missionaries in the frustrated and decadent Roman Empire, his version of the Faith, brought new

19

hope. In the early centuries the mainland British Kingdoms outside of Scotland had fallen under the Roman Empire: When the Romans left, these kingdoms defended themselves, viewing the Scots of Ireland and the Scots of Scotland as threatening barbarians; just as the Romans in Europe regarded the Germans and Slavs. In Britain these Irish barbarian invasions were contained on the west coast; but the British Celtic Kingdoms were eventually occupied by the Anglo-Saxons of Germanic origin, invading from the east coast: the Anglo-Saxons in turn were conquered by the Normans in 1066. The Anglo-Saxon Kingdoms were permanently united under the Normans, who overran the whole British Isles.

During the Roman occupation of Britain the power of Rome had gazed across the North Channel, and a number of trading expeditions had been made to *Hibernia*, from which hordes of barbarians launched their forces. The Romans had called the Irish *Scotus*. The Caesars decided that the frontiers of Rome should be the Elbe in Germany and Hadrian's Wall in northern Britain; and the Irish Sea. From the Isle of Man *(Mona)* they would have a convenient route; under a more advanced expedition, progress from northern England into Scottish Galloway, would have brought them opposite the Ulster coast, and easy access into present-day Antrim and Down, fighting the painted and long-haired Picts all the way. It was in this region, either in the Larne area or at Rathin Island (the shortest distance between Ireland and Scotland) that Man is said to have found a route to Ireland or Erin many thousands of years before Christ. Excavations at Larne in County Antrim in 1935, revealed a life style of naked fisher folk living on beaches, casting their nets and hunting with spears. They are said to represent Ireland's first inhabitants and were called the Larnian culture after the modern name of the town. Tradition states that the Gaels or Goidels, who came after the Stone Age people, came from Spain across the Spanish Sea, to land in the south west of Ireland: they were known also as the Milesians. The familiar scenario of later centuries, of

20

murder, rapine, conquest, integration and reconciliation was acted out as they took the place of the already existing culture. Like later invaders the Gaels never succeeded in totally overthrowing the primitives. The Gaels were successful outside Ulster, penetrating the broad rivers, the path of the Norsemen, to whom the Gaels fell victim themselves. In early Irish history, part myth and part fact, the Gaels of the south, led by Queen Maeve, subdued the north: Maeve's men were known as the "Men of Ireland", whilst the leaders of the north, descendants of the original primitives, were known as the "Men of Ulster". The "Men of Ulster" saw the Gaels or Goidels as an aristocratic warlike class that had only partially overcome the pre-Celtic community. The Gaels wished to build up and impose their own laws throughout Ireland. Underneath the Gaelic conquest always lay the brooding pre-Celtic tribes, and great tribal diversity within Gaeldom itself. The Gaels believed in petty tribal kingships, uniting into groups and provinces to defend common interests; thus by the fifth century there were several provincial kings holding sway over smaller statelets, but these may have formed the basis of the pre-Celtic community. In Ulster the local capital was *Emain Macha* or Navan Fort near Armagh. A nominal central authority, always resisted by the other kings, was established by the fifth century: this was the Ardriship, originating in the south and established at Tara, but often fought over by the north. The Brehons or professional lawyers interpreted the Gaelic laws. The Gaels and pre-Celts practised a form of Druidism; so from the start they had a lot in common. When the Christianity of Saint Patrick arrived in the fifth century the Druid culture was already many centuries old and coming near the peak of its contribution. Gaelic law ran throughout all of Ireland, as Ulster, conquered by the south about the fifth century, accepted the new ways. "National Assemblies" were held in the Boyne Valley with religious ceremonies and games, with buying and selling and general entertainment. However these "Irish Olympics" did not cover up the basic warring nature of Irish society, and unwillingness like other

European communities of the same age, to settle down under civilized order or a unified system. At the beginning of the Christian era the Kingdom of Connaught lay beyond the safe waters of the Shannon; to the north lay Ulster; then the north and the southern Leinster kingdoms; there was the south-west Kingdom of Munster, as remote as Ulster. Within these realms lay a crazy-quilt of tiny tribal regions that fought each other over territory, often sparked off over cattle raids.

SAINT PATRICK

Irish raids into Britain in the fourth century coincided with the spread of Christianity into Ireland. Succat or Patrick came to convert the Gaels, who practised a Druidism common to other European Celts. The Gaelic conquest in Ireland had reached its height, and had engulped the north. It has been said that Ireland, untouched by Imperial Rome, surrendered peacefully to spiritual Rome: however this may be far from the truth; from the beginning the Gaels moulded Christianity into their own traditions, putting faith in a Gaelic church, not acknowledging the Roman Calender until the tenth century; and through geographical circumstances lukewarm on the effective primacy of the Roman See. Practices in the Roman Church that became explicit as the original revelation proceeded, tended to be resisted in the far west of Christendom. At the close of the Roman World, the isolated island of Ireland - that might have eventually fallen under political Rome - had a chance to make one of the greatest contributions to Western Civilization. Saint Patrick's mission to Ireland, said to have started about 432 AD, had far reaching consequences for Christendom; it was Irish scholarship and Irish missionaries that provided one of the key dynamics behind the advance of European Catholicism. The debt that the Church of Rome owes Ireland - and Ulster, where tradition has it that Patrick was brought up, and where he established his see at Armagh - was perhaps epitomized when Pope John Paul II visited Eire in September 1979. Divisions between Protestants and Catholics in Ireland made the Pope unable to visit Armagh in Northern Ireland. The Church of Saint Patrick grew up in a tribal atmosphere used to highly complex territorial divisions brought about by family and clan feud. The Church was organized within leading families, compromising with local traditions that did not threaten Christianity. Whereas in Europe the Church was organized along the Roman Imperial "diocese" system, Saint Patrick is said to have appointed three-hundred bishops; but the eventual form of Primitive Christianity in Ireland was monastic, rather like the original Primitive Christianity of the Eastern deserts. The monastery gave monks and refugees protection from tribal feud. Little wooden huts were grouped in streets around a stone church, some centres like Bangor in County Down having as many as three-thousand monks working and chanting away. The abbot's rule was stern; he was elected by the family of the founder, bringing about considerable independence of the Roman Church. During the sixth and seventh centuries Ireland was free from invasions, which must account in large measure for the rapid growth of the Gaelic Church. The barbarian invasions that were breaking up Europe, gave Irish monasteries a chance to attract many scholars from abroad. This was the age of Glendalough in County Wicklow in the south and Bangor in the north.

Tradition has it that a slave brought to Ulster in one of the many *Scotti* raids into Britain suddenly turned the pagan, Druid-fearful Ulstermen of Antrim away from the magical powers of their masters. The Druids had for centuries looked to the stars, and had presided over secondary religions built around fairies, idols, fire, water and the Sun. They were advisers to the kings and tribal chieftains, and held a power similar to that of the medicineman in native American culture. They could be seen celebrating their rites in the stone temples, dressed in their white flowing habits. They were revered by the illiterate herdsmen of Antrim around Sliab Mis (Slemish) mountain, where Patrick became a slave and a swineherd. Only a day's journey away on foot, through dangerous territory, and falling from the great plateau of Antrim, lay the coast, and the North Channel, the land of the island sea kings. Sea gods and pagan idols and other symbols held sway. So remarkable was the later Ulster conversion and subsequent missions throughout Ireland, that it has been said that "there is no instance of any other nation that universally received it (Christianity) in so short a space of time as the Irish did" and "within a century of his death the Irish Church was itself sending out missionaries to foreign lands - to Scotland and Northern England, and then to Continental Europe, where they played a great part in the construction of Christendom after the breakdown of the Roman system under the barbarian invasions". After escaping from slavery in about 407 AD, Patrick is said to have returned to Ireland in 432 AD, perhaps to County Wicklow in the south, following in the footsteps of the earlier Palladius mission of 431 AD.

The hysteria engendered by the conversion of thousands of pagans was considerable; little glens and moorland hollows may have at first provided clandestine meeting places, whilst the mass conversions must have been frowned upon like "pop concerts" today by the ruling Druid classes. The crazed pagan, in the grip of the Druids, would rather hear Patrick's sermons; the peasants were exhorted to forsake their ancient gods and break with the Druids, who demanded human sacrifice. There may have been strong internal disruptive forces working within Paganism to bring about such spectacular conversions; Patrick may have been only one of the many Christian missionaries that attempted Irish conversion. They may have been killed in the early centuries after Christ by the primitive tribes. Patrick may have conveniently built upon the small measure of success of his predecessors. Tribal hysteria and following the leader was not a principle, or vice, unknown to the Pagan or Christian. The mass conversions of Patrick were built upon already existing religious principles, albeit of another kind.

The Ulster tradition is that Patrick or Succat was captured in a raid, probably into Wales, about 401 AD, but Irish raiders went as far away as Brittany in France. He was about sixteen years old, but already a Christian; he would therefore have learnt his Christianity from Roman missionaries in the Empire. He was sold as a slave, having to tolerate the vices and liberties with his person, which Paganism did not condemn. Modern research has it that Patrick came from Dumbarton in Argyll in Scottish Dalriada, and came to Ulster via the North Channel. Others say that he was taken to Connaught in the far west of Ireland; others that there were "two Patricks", one for the north and one for the south. It is undoubtedly true that he could have come as far away as Spain; or indeed that he was a Gael himself and never left Irish shores, and that Christianity came to Ireland from Roman-occupied Britain via trading expeditions;or that Patrick himself was unaware of his origins. Ireland may have been locally Christianized*during the first, second and third centuries, and not as traditionally supposed from the time of the later Roman missions. Patrick, or Succat, had spent his childhood as a Christian and as an Irish slave and then escaped to study a more sophisticated Christianity in Europe. The Ulster tradition is that he herded sheep around Slemish Mountain, which agrees with the findings of modern research, that Patrick came across the North Channel from Dumbarton from Scottish Dalriada. Slemish rears up like a green island amongst the purple moorlands and bright blue skies of Antrim. From here he could see the small islands and mulls of Scottish Dalriada, and ships sailing on the busy North Channel. He was enslaved to Lord Miliuc. Succat was a young man apart, barely controlling his urges to convert the pagans, to lead them from their excesses and immoralities. Like the evangelists in the Bible he heard in a dream, divinely inspired that a ship lay a hundred miles away to take him away from Ulster. This after six years in captivity. Providence

---

* Julian of Toledo says that the Apostle James addressed a canonical letter from Ireland to the Jews in Spain. James, the son of Zebedee - and St Paul - are cited by other authorities as having visited the "Western Islands".

dictated that Succat should take ship and prepare elsewhere for great missionary work. He may have decided that his mission was to convert the whole island to Christianity. Perhaps Succat escaped down the winding moorlands of the Antrim Plateau onto the coast near present-day Larne. He may have taken ship across the North Channel to Scottish Dalriada, taking advantage of a moment of tribal feud, in an effort to trace his parents in the Dumbarton region; or if the older tradition is accepted, then he may have taken ship or travelled by another route to North Wales. Certainly Patrick's six years in Ulster instilled within him great resolve, built around his own and Christianity's loathing of Paganism and its depraved rites and liberties.

Slavery was an important institution in Gaelic Ireland as elsewhere in the ancient world. Like oil and mechanical power today it formed the basis of power and energy, and like oil and mechanical power it was often abused. Human muscle and animal power were the foundations of society, which Patrick realized, as he performed his tasks. In his Confession, written to defend himself against criticism made by other missionaries in Ireland, he stated that "... the women who are kept in slavery suffer especially; they constantly endure even onto terrors and threats". Gaelic Christianity did not abolish slavery, or concubinage (the keeping of many wives). Slaves were still chained up and the bondage nature of the institution made women slaves especially prized. Like cattle, slaves were an acceptable means of payment: it is likely that Succat was "sold" into Antrim in return for payment for other services. Slaves were a measure of value and an acceptable means of payment. A conventional rate of exchange was established between female slaves and cattle: six strong heifers or three milch cows were the equivalent of a female slave.

Succat or Patrick was in his forties when he decided to return to Ireland. He had left about 407 AD, studying at several famous monastic schools on the Continent, which included Tours, Lerins and Auxerre. He had learnt that Palladius's mission of 431 AD had failed. About twenty-five years elapsed between Patrick escaping from captivity and him landing again, probably somewhere in the Wicklow region in the south of Ireland. By now he had been consecrated bishop. Patrick, the patrician, as his name implies, came to the initially hostile Gaels. He was now well-informed about the culture of the Roman world; he was no illiterate evangelical fired with irrational vision; for his mission could be ranked with that of Saint Paul. No literati, Patrick could however write interesting Latin. Great changes had taken place within Gaelic society. Patrick came to Ireland with a Bible and New Testament that had only recently taken shape; many of the more "questionable" books of the New Testament, for example the Book of Revelation, had been condemned by the Early Church as heretical; but had later been received as authoritative. The doctrine of Papal Primacy had not yet become fully explicit in the life of the Church; the doctrines of Transubstantation and the Assuption of the Blessed Virgin Mary were unknown to these primitive Catholics in their modern form. The Christianity Patrick established has been claimed by the Church of Ireland of today to be trully "Protestant", whilst Roman Catholics look to Patrick as a true Catholic living at the beginning of the Christian tradition: the Church, moulded by history, and guided by the doctrines of Rome and the precedents of the Church fathers, would later attempt to express the True Faith in such dogmas as the Assumption and the Infallibility of the Pope. Patrick had received his mandate from the Pope in 432, which is good enough for Catholics; whilst he was not aware of such doctrines as the Assumption of the Virgin Mary, which is good enough for Protestants. Patrick, however, lived in a Roman world full of heresies that have sprung up in all ages to combat Papal Primacy, at times affecting the Papacy itself. Certainly Patrick's early gospel to Ireland was simple by necessity and relatively uninvolved.

Patrick came to Ireland when the Pagan World was everywhere in decadence; old gods were being replaced with new ones. Whilst there is no evidence that Ireland had other than trading contacts with the Roman Empire, it is difficult to conceive that she was totally isolated as is the traditional view: movements that were taking place in Europe were afoot in Ireland as well: Antrim Dalriada had been expanding into Argyll since the early part of the Christian era; Antrim and Scottish Dalriada was a Druid thalassocracy and was one of the many kingdoms to be evangelized by Patrick. The general Christian Civilization that took root in the north was as sophisticated as the one that took root in the south in the fifth to seventh centuries. However the southern tradition states that Christianity may have come to Ireland via the Spanish Sea from the Iberian peninsula, following the path of the Gaelic invasions of about 700 BC, which would agree with the view that Patrick capitalized on the success of much earlier missionaries, in view of the speed of his conversions. Like the Germans of the Roman Empire, the men of Dalriada and Ulaid, or the Gaels, never became conquered by Rome. Rome was at her fullest military extent by the first century. Like the Huns and German barbarians, the Irish kingdoms came under the influence of Rome by virtue of the fear of conquest by her. Christianity came to Ireland, as it did to the barbarians of Northern Europe, as a revitalizing force; something that the historian Edward Gibbon claimed had destroyed Imperial Rome. The new spiritual Rome was not supposed to be an empire at all: it was the Papacy, by the ninth century claiming rule over Christendom, from the Eastern deserts to the wastes of Donegal. It was a primitive Catholicism, very "Protestant" in character without the sophistication of the Medieval fathers.

Patrick proceeded into the north of Ireland, to the Kingdom of Dál Fiatach (Present-day Eastern Down). At its capital, Lecale, he was treated as in Wicklow, with hostility by the native chieftains; but legend has it that Dichu, Lord of Lecale, became overwhelmed by Patrick's arguments, and succumbed to his personality and to Christianity. Patrick's role is cast like Aaron's in the river-god world of Egypt, sometimes mesmerizing Pharoah, and always aware that Pharoah could turn upon him; or discover his slave origins and send him back to herd cattle. His greatest hope was to convert the princes and to anoint the bishops. He returned south, having gained a foothold in the north, to ancient Tara, seat of the "Emperors of Ireland", the *Árd Rí*, and appealed to the whole Gaelic nations. It was Easter when he reached the hill of Tara. Night fell and Patrick lit a paschal fire: to the Druids, Patrick had broken the ancient law, for during the Council of Tara, at which the family princes discussed the affairs of the island, no other fires except the huge fire of Tara was to burn. The Druids demanded that Patrick himself should be burnt forthwith, bringing his mission to nothing. Like Aaron before Pharaoh he outdid the chief magicians by the strength of his "magic" and subtlty of his argument: in the dying pagan world there were other men with as much eloquence and better powers than established figures. The people were following Patrick and his new religion: the princes should be converted to maintain power over the people; the wicked Druids should be shunned. Patrick proceeded to destroy the idols and totems and sex symbols of paganism. It is said that at one meeting he baptized twelve thousand. However elements of Druidism prevailed, for Christian festivals were often made to coincide with the Druid's sacred days: Easter now coincided with the rites that heralded the coming of Spring; sacred wells that sprang up along winding roads and byways could be blessed and their water used as "holy" in church services. The Druid temple might become the Christian Church. Although most of Patrick's missions were outside Ulster, he is said to have made his way north again in 455 AD, to make Armagh the primary see of Ireland. Armagh was a monastery set upon a hill, but after Patrick's death it was disputed to be the primatial see. Patrick, undoubtedly regarding himself as the chief bishop of the whole island under mandate of Rome, was also aware that he would have competitors from within Christianity itself. He did not establish a "national" church: the average prince or herdsman regarded their own position in Ireland as the average citizen of Britain today might regard his place in Europe: without definite unity, or political form, and without nationality. After the Gaelic conquest Ireland veered to a common Gaelic language. Undoubtedly Patrick travelled throughout the length and breadth of Ireland, often riding in a chariot, risking the hostility of the Druids, and establishing shrines.

It is said that at Lough Derg in County Donegal Patrick spent forty days and forty nights in fasting and prayer in a mysterious cave on the island in the Red Lake, as Lough Derg has been called. The island lies half a mile from the shore: it became known as Patrick's Purgatory. However Armagh lingers on as the great centre of Saint Patrick in Ireland, shut off from Eire as a result of Partition in modern times, but still ruling the whole Protestant and Roman Catholic population of Ireland. Its pre-eminence has been attested from the seventh century, but it was not officially recognized as the Primitial See until 1152. Its significance probably lies in its strategic position: it is two miles to the west of the ancient hill fortress "capital" of Ulster, *Emain Macha* or Navan Fort. Saul in County Down has been claimed as both the landing place and burial place of Patrick. In the grounds of the now Protestant Church of Ireland Cathedral at Downpatrick there is a large granite boulder inscribed with a cross and the name PATRIC. It was in the Downpatrick region that he first converted the Chieftain of Lecale; and perhaps he returned to die there in 461 AD. The truth is that we know very few facts about Saint Patrick or about the strength and determination of the Roman mission. Certainly there have been no snakes seen in Ireland, either north or south, for legend has it that Patrick drove them all out in the fifth century.

BEFORE CHRIST

Authorities differ about early Man's origins in Ireland; but it may be imagined that from the Mull of Kintyre in Scotland early Stone Age man could see the beckoning white cliffs of Antrim in the area of Rathlin Island. Crossing the twelve mile stretch and probing inland to Lough Neagh up the River Bann, they found eels, salmon and waterfoul in enormous quantities. Here their wattled huts, preserved in the earth, have been dated to 700-4000 BC: they penetrated westwards to Upper and Lower Lough Erne in Fermanagh and down the broad waters of the Shannon. The world of Saint Patrick, forty-eight generations displaced from the year 2000 AD, was far more remote to the age of the great megalith builders of prehistoric Ulster. These ancient nature worshippers, knowing nothing of Judaism or monotheism, left perhaps as great an impact on the community as any of the later invaders. Scientists say that blood tests in the north and west of Ulster show that there are a greater number of people having Blood Group O, which is a strong pre-Celtic and pre-Gaelic characteristic. It is reckoned that the south of Ireland during the Stone Age was left largely unpeopled by these fisher folk: to the primitive mind, in the south lay primeval woodlands, inhabited by monstrous gods and invisible supernatural armies that might threaten the existence of early Man in the north. The south in fact is thought to have been inhabited by a separate band of tomb builders that came from Spain. Geographically the north of Ireland is a region of course that stretches outside the confines of the later province of Ulster: it can best be imagined by geographically dividing Ireland in half, east to west. These fisher folk penetrated as far south as the Boyne Valley, living on the edge of the world, singing songs about the terrors of the deep south. Their great megalith court graves are dominating features in the north. Over a thousand examples have been found, occuring in a line from Clew Bay in Donegal to Dundalk Bay on the east coast. The megaliths were not only the burial grounds of the roving

31

chieftains, but were associated with human fertility and crops.

In early geological times (the Tertiary period), the Antrim Coast was the scene of gigantic volcanic eruptions; it was part of the Scottish-Islandic volcanic complex. Great headlands embracing sweeping bays must have overawed early man. At the Giant's Causeway in the north of the coast, igneous material hit the sea at great rate, forming gigantic crystals, a phenomenon repeated across the North Channel at Staffa in Scotland. The chalk and limestone and flints of the Antrim Coast were thus capped and preserved from denudation: it was these white cliffs, glistening with flint and capped by black igneous stone that must have awed early man on the Mull of Kintyre. The white cliffs of Antrim are a great rarity in Atlantic Europe. Flints were useful for the points of spears and the tips of arrows and for making fire on the broad desolate beaches. These flints were fine-grained sedimentaries, hardened by igneous contact, and ideal for the head of an axe: this was the "bluestone" of Tievebulliagh, a pointed peak near present-day Rathin Island. Between 3500-2000 BC the primeval tribes exported stone axes from Tievebulliagh throughout the`British Isles - about one hundred and sixty generations ago.

Geography from the beginning demarcated the north of Ireland from the south. At the end of the Ice Age, the great glaciers retreated north: they dumped drumlins or rounded hills of boulder clay up to half a mile long and a hundred feet high, providing obstacles to drainage and communication in a great loop that runs roughly between the south of County Donegal to County Down. The border country of Ulster was therefore always difficult to settle; this together with the east of Ulster's proximity to north-west Scotland has provided the religiously divided Ulsterman with facts justifying a political position separate from the rest of Ireland. Man may first have settled in the north of Ireland, probably in the Larne region, and that the civilization of pre-Celtic Ireland was handed onto the whole island through the north; it is also true that the Gaelic Church became established in the north, and that Saint Patrick may have been a more northward looking than a southern orientated evangelist. At the height of Gaelic Christian Civilization, in the sixth and seventh centuries, the centre of culture moved to the south, as ecclesiastical centres like Glendalough in County Wicklow became world renowned and havens of learning. The Gaelic origins of the Church are claimed by Ulster and by the monks of Dalriada and by Saint Columba of Derry, who flourished in the sixth century.

Celtic tribes began to reach Ireland somewhere after 600 BC, a movement of warriors that had begun somewhere around 700 BC from a cradle north of the Alps. The Celts mingled with and conquered the earlier fisher folk and stone builders, bringing with them a superior civilization based on metal: the stone axe was as remote from the metal axe as the bow and arrow is to the gun. The Celts built defensive earth works and lake dwellings, a characteristic that persisted well into early Christian times. The hill fort of *Emain Macha* mear Armagh is thought to be dated from the third century BC, and to have been abandoned about 332 AD, as a result of the raid made by Queen Maeve of Connaught, at the head of the High-Kingship (Emperorship) of Ireland. The Celts now became the Gaelic aristocratic warriors. They feared revolt by the pre-Celtic subjects or the Fir Bolgs. The Gaelic Kingdoms united to help crush revolt. The "Men of Ulster" represented the last stronghold of the Fir Bolgs in this latter day primeval world, full of moorland mists and fiery sunsets, on the island the Romans thought lay on the very edge of the world. Ulstermen were driven back by the arrogant Gaels or Goidels; the Fir Bolgs built the "Great Wall of Ulster", reaching from Newry in south-east County Down to Lough Erne on the border of Donegal. The "Men of Ulster" were cornered. Tara, near Dublin, became the "capital" of the Goidels and "capital" of Ireland: here the great festival *(feis)* of Tara, presided over by the Irish Goidel Emperors or *Árd Rís* ruling their loose confederacy, lasted until the Norman conquest in 1169. In the fourth century AD the "Men of Ireland" marched north at the head of a great army against the Wall of

Ulster and slew Fergus the last king of the pre-Gaelic north. The fight to survive was not yet over. The "Men of Ulster" retreated east across the Bann, hurrying in their currachs across Lough Neagh, to hold out in present-day Antrim and Down: this they called the Kingdom of Ulidia, and relations were strengthened with Scottish Dalriada and the Sea Kingdoms to keep the warring Goidels at bay. The rest of Ulster was divided amongst the victors and they took their place in this unique phase of Irish unity, looking south to Tara near Dublin as the capital. North-west Ulster fell under the men of Gaelic blood: it became known as the Northern Kingdom: its capital was Aileach, a great stone-built cashel on a hill north-west of present-day Derry. The Northern Kingdom, which lay west of Lough Neagh, was Gaelic Ulster; whilst the "Men of Ulster" in Antrim and Down were of an older and prouder race: they had formed a combination based upon the old pre-Celtic chieftains and felt themselves under siege, as the Goidels, who had overrun other parts of the British Isles in the general Celtic movement, established the Ardriship. From the Northern Kingdom of Aileach were descended the great O'Neills of Central Ulster and Tyrone. The Gaelic Northern Kingdom conquered Ulidia (present-day Antrim and Down) by 1000 AD. The reorganization of the north prompted fresh migrations from Antrim Dalriada and from Down: this had started in 470 AD when Fergus Mac Erc, prince of Dalriada in North Antrim and his three brothers crossed the North Channel and founded the Kingdom of Argyll (or the Eastern Gael); they followed in the footsteps of centuries of intercourse between the north-east of Ireland and the west of Scotland. This was also the age of the expansion of the Gaelic Church in the north, the age of Saint Patrick and the dawning of the age of Saint Columba, who had an "international" outlook.

THE GAELIC CHURCH

In 563 AD Columba (or Colum Cille) a native prince of Derry on the banks of the Foyle, in the Northern Gaelic Kingdom, had turned from a warlike existence to follow Christianity. Later he established a monastery on the island of Iona, off the coast of Argyll. Before his death in 597AD Columba became known as the "Abbot-Bishop of the Isles"; he became the apostle of Scotland; whilst Saint Patrick, who had died in 461 AD, with his see at Armagh, in the south of Ulster, was perhaps a northward looking man. In 548 AD a terrible plague hit Ireland, and the misery ensuing undoubtedly helped to set off a new wave of migrations that started between north-eastern Ulster and Scottish Argyll. During times of plague and general calamity a monastery was a haven and a repository of learning. Islands such as Iona and Skellig Michael (in south-west Ireland), provided isolation not only from plague but from the more immediate consequences of native wars. Nearly all the founders of these monasteries were aristocratic Gaels, warriors who had conquered Ireland from the megalith builders. On Iona monks like Columba, an ex-Druid, could follow their own rigorous Gaelic rites within the Church: it was not until the seventh century that the Gaelic Church came into line with the Roman Church on the date of Easter. On Iona Columba spent eleven years of his life, whilst the rest was spent in bringing Christianity to the barbaric Picts of Argyll and Galloway. Like the Druids the disciples of Christ were reputed to hold supernatural powers: Adoman, Abbot of Iona (688-704 AD), who succeeded Columba, wrote in his *Life of Columba* that the saint had prophetic revelations, performed miracles and saw visions.

The monastery of Iona was a purely family affair: all the first twelve abbots, except for two, came from the same family: it was not only a monastery but a little state within itself, amongst the island realms off the west coast of Scotland. Married laymen lived with the monks and worked the land. Irish monasticism, unlike the Continental Roman tradition, was not so formally organized: it reflected the background and traditions of the warrior lords who received the gospel and went forth with sword and scriptures from these ascetic communities. Iona, more than other monasteries, extended its monastic "empire": Iona controlled monasteries in both Scotland and Ireland, the abbots making regular visits to them. This was the monastery's *paruchia* owing allegiance to the *comarba* or abbot. In the sixth and seventh centuries the abbots soon superseded the authority of the bishops, giving the Gaelic Church a distinctly monastic character. The monks were great documenters, so the history of the seventh century is quite well known. Continuous year by year annals were kept at Iona, and probably at Bangor in County Down.

Columba was one of the "twelve apostles of Ireland", who had studied under Clonard Finnian. Clonard Finnian, a southern saint, had founded a monastery at Clonard on the borders of the kingdoms of Meath and Leinster, lying directly south of Ulster. Columba was said to have been descended from Niall of the Nine Hostages, the great Druid raider from Ulster, whose *Scotti* raided Britain at the beginning of the fifth century; and also descended from Loarn, head of Scottish Dalriada. Columba was born at Gartan in County Donegal, and his cousin was High-King or Irish Emperor. Columba is said to have done most of his studies in the south of Ireland, at Dublin and of course at Clonard. It was in an oak grove that this Gaelic warrior, turned gentle Christian, founded his first monastery, calling it Doire or Oakwood. Tradition has it that Oakwood occupied the site of the present Protestant Cathedral of Londonderry; whilst others say that it occupied the site the Roman Catholic Cathedral, inside and outside the walls of Derry respectively. If it was founded outside the walls it would have been on the marshy ground now occupied by the Roman Catholic Bogside of the City, scene of great lamentation in the twentieth century. Oakwood (Doire), whence the name Derry arose, was Columba's favourite monastery; whilst out of his three Irish foundations Kells and Durrow are the others. During the great age of Christian art and learning the monastery of Kells produced the famous Book of Kells, the Gospels written beautifully in the handwriting of the monks. The art of writing had appeared in Ireland with the introduction of Christianity, so Columba and his monks were the harbingers of a new technology. The Book of Kells is now preserved in the Library of Trinity College, Dublin. It is said that Columba had a dual nature, even after his conversion: in a fit of temper, after an argument with the King of Tara in the south, he - Columba- as a warrior lord - called upon his tribe to wage war. Three thousand were slaughtered in County Sligo. As a penance Columba was ordered to leave Ireland forever and preach the gospel overseas, where he could gain as many souls as were lost in the battle. In disgrace Columba set off with twelve friends in a small currach, travelling to Iona, deep into the waters of the north: upon reaching Iona, he had travelled to one of the last outposts in Argyll on the borders of Pictish territory.Perhaps there is little truth in this legend about Columba's argument with the King of Tara; but his voyage to Iona is venerated and repeated by the faithful each year as they sail forth, making the hazardous voyage, as their saint did, in open boats. Columba however returned to Ireland several times as a political emissary of Scottish Dalriada. Columba may have been following in the footsteps of several monks who took to the sea in this period: Saint Brendan of Clonfert, popularly known as Brendan the Navigator, is said to have taken ship and sailed to the lost world of the west, present-day America, from south-west Ireland in the latter part of the fifth century. Monks like Columba and Brendan represented the more practical and civilized form of monasticism. Many early Christians found convenient refuges in isolated spots: they were solitary figures known as anchorites, sitting sometimes for years in a single position, on top of rocks or occupying caves and beaches. They contemplated the new religion, forgetting about the conflicts of the Druid way of life.

At a time when the Anglo-Saxon invaders of Britain, coming

37

from Germany, were destroying Christianity, Saint Patrick (*circa* 432) and Saint Columba (*circa* 563) were establishing and organizing it in Ireland, based from Armagh in Ulster and Iona in Scottish Dalriada. In the monastic age , the monasteries spread out from the north down the east coast of Ireland and into the central plain, to be founded by secluded river banks and in pleasant oakwoods; into island retreats like Iona in Scotland and Skellig Michael in south-west Ireland. When the Norsemen arrived in the late eighth century a good deal of Ireland had turned from paganism; but it is not at all conclusive that the greater multitude accepted Christianity for any length of time; since modern historians believe that the round towers, said to have been built to withstand the Norse onslaught, were used as much to protect Gaelic Christian foundations against Gaelic pagan raiders. Christianity was accepted by the warrior classes, for it provided an effective focus of organization and a new system that would reinvigorate the old pagan world that was everywhere disintegrating, but paganism arrived again like a hurricane from Norway and Sweden to challenge the Faith. The disciples of Columba, having Chritianized the leaders of the Picts, had then a convenient base to move into northern England and its pagan kingdoms: here the Gaels would find the remnants of Roman Christianity, which would later assert itself as spiritual Rome started to influence Europe's new barbarian leaders. From Columba's humble monastery at Iona, a chain of monasteries was established that stretched through Burgundy in France, to Saxony in Germany and Bobbio in Italy. Irish monks made a base at Lindisfarne in Northumbria. It was not until the Synod of Whitby in 664 AD that the Irish were bound to accept the new spiritual Roman system. It was not only by the early eighth century that Iona itself and the north of Ireland looked to the Vicar of Rome as Universal Pope of the Holy Catholic Church. The pressure of the Norse attacks (Iona fell in 830 AD) may have helped to persuade the Gaelic Church to look to Rome, if only for survival. The Norse attacks were to cut north-eastern Ulster and Scottish Dalriada apart.

Columba returned to Ulster in 575 AD for the Convention of Druim Cett, now that all was forgiven him in the Northern Kingdom; with him came the King of Dalriada; this was twelve years after the founding of Iona. Druim Cett was a "national" Council of Ireland of kings and abbots, and it met in present-day County Londonderry. The relations between Scotland and Ireland were in dispute, particularly the role that Antrim Dalriada should play in Irish affairs. It was decided that Scottish Dalriada should give its military services to the High-King of Ireland and his Scottish vassals, and its naval service to the King of Argyll. The capital of Scottish Dalriada was at Loarn, near present-day Dumbarton, said to be Saint Patrick's birthplace. Columba spoke to the Convention of Druim Cett about the problems posed by the conquest of Paganism by Christiantiy: the native bards or poets (*Fili*) had been wandering minstrels, carrying within them a rich Gaelic tradition of paganism, some of which was adapted to suit Christianity. They consented to follow Christianity; but they were prone to preach subversion against the gospel and to lead the Gaels back into the Druid fold. It was proposed that the bards or *Fili* should be banished; but Columba's casting vote in the Convention of Druim Cett saved them from oblivion, turning them into full time Christians. Columba, perhaps mindful of his own Druid past, advised that each of the province kings should have a poet to preserve the ancient ways, and to hand Gaelic traditions on to coming generations. The Order of Poets survived until 1603, when the Gaelic earls of Ulster submitted to England. Columba carried within him the traditions of previous ages, and attempted to reconcile the Christian with the Pagan world: this was the policy of the Primitive Catholic Church elsewhere in Europe and the East. Columba died in 597 AD: not only had he brought Gaelic Christianity to parts of northern England, but also the Gaelic language, which however died out with the imposition of the Latin Roman rites. Irish monks reached as far south in England as East Anglia and Glastonbury. In northern

39

Northumbria its kings spoke Irish for about one hundred years. The defeat of Armagh over the date of Easter and over the tonsure (the shaving off of the front of the monks' hair) did not affect its primacy over the Irish Church in general. By the ninth century the self-styled supremacy of Armagh over the Catholic Church in Ireland was affirmed. An ancient canon in the *Book of Armagh* states that "whensoever any cause that is very difficult and unknown to all the judges of the Scottic nation shall arise, it should rightly be referred to the See of the Archbishop of the Irish, to wit Patrick, and the examination of the prelate thereof, but if by him and his wise men such a cause cannot be determined, we have decreed that it shall be sent to the Apostolic See, that is, to the Chair of the Apostle Peter which has authority of the City of Rome". The declining state of the post-Roman world made referals to Rome difficult; whilst the successors of Saint Patrick may have preferred to settle religious disputes among themselves. Rome from the Apostolic Age, claimed primacy over the material and spiritual World; and other churches, over which she had leadership by the ninth century, followed in the face of the majority. However today Protestants in Northern Ireland often point out that whilst the "Chair of Peter" is mentioned in the documents of the Early Church, it is unlikely that the Catholic Church of Patrick or Columba regarded the Bishop of Rome as the ultimate earthly authority or that his word in Church matters was absolute; or that the Bishop of Rome regarded himself, at this date, in this respect. Catholics reply, in response to Protestant claims that later doctrines such as Transubstantiation were unknown to the Gaelic Church, that Papal Primacy is implicit in the original revelation given to the Church; and as Christ's Mission proceeded, they became explicit in the life of the Church; the epitomization of this attitude being the promulgation of Papal Infallibility by Pope Pius IX in 1869. Some Protestant sects deny the authority of bishops and veer to the belief that Patrick and Columba were themselves sinking into error, and were definitely Rome-centred, and were probably tainted with as much Paganism as with Roman Christianity.

The monastery of Bangor, said to have been one of the great launching pads for the European missions, had an independent rule of its own. Saint Comgall, founder of Bangor, was born at Maghermourne in County Antrim; the monastery of Bangor attracked monks from all over Europe, who must have arrived in their small boats, sailing up present-day Belfast Lough, to what is today a modern seaside resort. Bangor was devastated by the Danes in 824 AD and it is said that over three-thousand monks were slain. Like Iona on the Atlantic shores of western Scotland, little remains of it today. Clonmacnois in County Offaly in southern Ireland was founded by Saint Ciaran, said to have been of humble birth and born at Larne in eastern County Antrim. Clonmacnois was pillaged several times and finally ceased to exist after Cromwell's soldiers sacked it in 1552. By 800 AD, when the Emperor Charlemagne had wielded large portions of Central Europe into a unified tribal Empire under spiritual guidance of Rome, the Gaels had established Christian Civilization firmly on the foundations of Irish Druidism. Whether the north of Ireland shone greater in this period of ecclesiastical expansion than the south of Ireland is perhaps an unfair comparison to make.

Part Two

NORSE AND NORMANS

THE NORSEMEN

The Norse never succeeded in conquering Ireland. Their kingdoms, pagan until they were driven out, lay on the eastern seaboard - amongst them the Kingdom of Dublin, the City of Wexford and the Norse City of Cork. As they took control of the North Channel about 795 AD, Scottish Dalriada was cut off from Antrim Dalriada. From the ninth and tenth centuries Argyll and the surrounding islands to the north and south started to develop a sense of independence under their new overlords. Orkney and Shetland were first of all to fall to these barbarians. The Norseman was a 'Finn-gall' or 'fair foreigner' from Norway, the most numerous invaders; the Dane was a 'Dubh-gall' or 'dark foreigner'. They rushed up the beaches, raiding monasteries, and slaughtering the inhabitants. An ancient prayer exclaimed: Good Lord, deliver us from the might of the men in the longships! The Norsemen are said to have arrived at Rathlin Island in Antrim Dalriada; they sailed down the Antrim Coast as the native chiefs watched helplessly. The Gaels, who had now overrun Antrim and Down, were appalled to see their kingdom divided. The rest of Ulster lay open to Norse attacks. The Norse had also attacked Ireland from the south-west, sailing out in a great curve from Norway, braving the waters of the Atlantic. They entered Ireland by its "back door" - rowing up the Shannon estuary, into the broad River Shannon itself, and into the Christian heartland of Ireland;

Their brightly coloured ships reached *Mona* (Anglo-Saxon *Maeng*) or the Isle of Man in the Irish Sea. The Norsemen were rovers and traders and were loath to pay tribute to their homeland; but the kings of Norway claimed tribute over Shetland and the Inner Hebrides until the late Middle Ages. In 830 AD the Abbot of Iona and his monks had fled down the North Channel in their flimsy ships and landed in the Ards Peninsula, to take refuge at Downpatrick, the ancient shrine of Saint Patrick; but it was to Armagh, still disputed as having absolute authority in Ireland, that the Gaelic Church rallied. Iona of course was a Gaelic patrimony that might have competed with Armagh or Rome, and some day set up an independent Gaelic Papacy of its own. During Columba's lifetime(521-597)·Scottish Dalriada rose to dominate Antrim Dalriada, Dunadd becoming the established political capital. The men of Antrim had swept far into the Pictish Highlands of Scotland: they were the *Scotti*, and, as their territory extended, they gave their name to the future Kingdom of Scotland. The original Antrim homeland became overshadowed as the Scottish colonies under Kenneth McAlpin started to build up the Kingdom of Scotland. Gaelic Ireland had extended her cultural sphere. Antrim Dalriada was now forced to take her place amongst the other kingships of Ulster; but the men of Antrim were still considered by the Gaels, and considered themselves, to be "Gall-Gaels", more akin to the men of the Isles. When neighbouring chieftains launched attacks upon Antrim Dalriada the "Gall-Gaels" would cry across the North Channel, despite the new Norse overlords. Although Dalriada and its associated lordships suffered considerably under the Norse, it was the southern Irish kingships, and the Gaels of Central Ulster, that were to show most resistance to them. The men of Antrim and the men of the Isles had a sea-based empire; they had much in common with the Norse, despite the Norse belief in Almighty Thor. However generally in Ireland outside the isolated Norse kingdoms, intermarriage between the Norse and the native community was possible; intermarriage was most marked in Scottish Dalriada and the Hebridean lordships.

In 919 all of Ulster, Meath and Connaught united to rid Ireland of the Norse Kingdoms; but the Irish were repulsed near Dublin; the Norse now extended their power from Dublin to the east, to join their other forces at Shannon and Limerick in the west. Norsemen and Danes of course would also fight amongst each other, bringing the date of their expulsion closer. At last Brian Boru was able to make a progress through all of Ireland, to Armagh in Ulster, as Scots-Irish Emperor. Irish and Scottish Dalriada was obliged to support Brian Boru in Ireland's fight against the Norsemen. At Armagh Brian heard Mass and laid twenty ounces of gold as a gift upon the altar. It is said that in the early part of the ninth century the pagans had overthrown the altar of Christ, turning the Cathedral into the Temple of Thor. In the *Book of Armagh*, a Latin scribe wrote that: "The holy Patrick, when going to Heaven, ordained that the whole fruit of his labour as well of baptism as of church matters and alms should be paid to the apostolic city which in Irish is called Ardmacha. So have I found it among the book of the Scots and have written it in the sight of Brian, emperor of the Scots, and what I have written he has confirmed for all the Kings of Cashel".

Brian Boru, a Gaelic warrior from the south of Ireland, was claiming an Empire over all the Gaels: over the Gaels who had left Antrim for Argyll, who had colonized Pictland, and who had now established the Kingdom of the Scots. Brian's Emperorship was in response to the grave Norse pressures, which now threatened to extinguish Gaelic Civilization and submerge the squabbling kingdoms of Gaelic Scotland and Gaelic Ireland. By 1000 AD the Gaels of Ireland and the rising kingdom of Scotland had a common racial stem, but were developing different political institutions to cope with external pressures and internal needs: in Ireland a loose confederacy, with whom Scottish Dalriada and north-east Ulster took their place in the need to unite around a common Norse enemy; in the south the warring kingships normally looked to Tara and the traditions of the Irish Gaels: the Gaelic Law was more carefully preserved in both the north and the south of Ireland than in the rising Scottish clanships. Norse invasions and general internal feud had deeper roots in Ireland generally, for Gaelic Scotland was determined on unity, with only a land border with England to the south. Links were strong between the northern and eastern coasts of Ulster with the kingdom of Scotland: this could either be a bridgehead or an obstacle to a Scots-Irish Empire. Brian Boru's dream of a unified Scots-Irish Empire rested therefore upon the unsteady foundations of clanship that the Anglo-Saxon Kings in England, under Alfred, and later the Normans, were crushing in their own country, placing in their stead a strong central monarchy. The feudal lords were in subservience. In Ireland the Scots-Irish Empire was divided between north and south; Malachy, who was originally joint Emperor with Brian, looked after the north. Iona was now deserted. Armagh, which Brian Boru venerated, was left under the north. Personal tragedy however was to rupture this would-be tribal Empire that could be likened to the earlier Charlemagne Federation of Germanic tribes in the ninth century. Kormlada, as the Norse called her, who controlled the Kingdom of Leinster, was at separate times Brian's and Malachy's wife: she decided to sell out to the north, to bring about Brian's fall. Brian besieged Dublin from September to Christmas 1013, but had to draw back. Kormlada now conspired with the Earl of Orkney, Sigurd, who stormed down the North Channel with two-thousand Norsemen clad in medieval mail: he was offered the bait of the Kingdom of Ireland and of course the hand of the beautiful, and treacherous Kormlada. Vikings took ship from the Isle of Man, bringing with them their huge axes. Brian Boru, now an old man, with the support of most of the Irish Kingdoms (except Kormlada's Leinster), defeated the Norsemen on Good Friday, 23 April 1014. Brian himself was too old to take part in the battle; but nevertheless his head was split open by a Viking axe as he rested in his tent. The Norsemen fled to their ships at Clontarf in the north of Dublin, where most of both men and ships perished at high tide. Of the treacherous Kormlada nothing is known; but it was to Armagh, now becoming firmly established by the turn of the century as the Primatial See, that Brian's body was borne. He was buried at the High Altar. Malachy died in 1022, and brought to an end the northern leadership that had lasted for six centuries. Scotland had been lukewarm on the dream of a united Gaelic Monarchy; but it was not to be forsaken: it would later be held up as a threat to Norman England, when Robert Bruce became King of Scotland. England fell under the Normans in 1066. The Normans were themselves of Viking descent, but they had accepted

48

Christianity. In 1169, the Normans invaded Ireland.

The islands and coasts of Dalriada and the Hebrides were still the haunt of Norse pirates, whom neither the Irish Kings or the Scots Kings could contain. The Norse pirates were still confident that the power of Norway might help re-establish their sway. They ruled their island strongholds, terrorizing Dalriada in their galleys. The Norse, Somerled, called himself King of the Gall-Gaels or Lord of Argyll. He was the ancestor of the MacDonnells of the Isles, who later crossed the North Channel to settle at Glenarm on the Antrim Coast in the later Middle Ages. The Kings of Norway had not forgotton their Scots and Irish vassals.Magnus "Barefoot", Sea-King of Norway sailed down the Atlantic in 1102 to collect tribute from the Hebrides. He then sailed down the North Channel to the Isle of Man. On his way back he landed to forage in Ulster, where he was slain by a local levy in 1103.

CATHOLICISM AND PAGANISM

The Catholic Church, based at Rome, was now steadily building up its temporal power and sought to bring the whole British Isles within its absolute authority. Where local political power was uncertain of uniting around a lasting central base, the Catholic Church could step in to provide a much needed social fusion. She supported local traditions, provided these did not try to control her: she incorporated the Roman Emperor's ability to rule local chieftains, and to let them cherish their own traditions as long as they rendered onto Caesar. But great corruption, which often goes with an extension of temporal authority, was spreading throughout the Church: the Gaelic Church was no exception. The whole Gaelic world was in conflict with the new culture brought in by the Norman invasions: they brought with them the sophistication of French Civilization; they were convinced in the Holy Catholic Church's universal mission, and to help purge Christendom of material corruption. With the Normans the

Middle Ages proper begin. They came to Ireland in 1169 in response to the breakdown of the Gaelic Confederacy and in response to the Normans' natural expansionist ambitions throughout the British Isles, particularly into Wales, giving them a springboard to Ireland and to the Wexford region. They would strengthen the influence of the Roman Church on the Gaelic lords. But the Normans never successfully penetrated the north. Their political power was confined to Antrim and Down. Carrickfergus on the shores of Belfast Lough became the chief stronghold in Ulster.

By the eleventh century the Catholic Church was determined upon self-reform, before heresy might provide an alternative purge. Gregory VII became Pope in 1073. Bishops were to be elected; synods were to be held, simony was to be eradicated; and loose living clerics were to be dealt with. Gregory VII developed the right to excommunicate and he did not hesitate to use it, in particular against the German Kings, to purify and maintain the unity of Christendom. In Ireland the bishops were attached to individual families from Saint Patrick's time. A good deal of the pre-Christian Gaelic culture was prevalent in the life of the Church. Slavery, as in many other countries, was still received by the Church, but the Medieval practice of serfdom was taking its place; whilst usury, until the age of Capitalism, was anathema. Saint Columba's old foundation at Derry had fallen into decay and was reformed. In Dalriada, as elsewhere, it is difficult to believe that the Druid influence did not persist alongside that of Christianity and that the pastoral gods of Antrim did not provide the Gaelic soul, as he looked out across the deep blue of the North Channel to Scotland, with a longing after the old idols. The Christian God might be only a temporary lord. Beltaine, or May Day, was still celebrated in the Antrim Hills and of course eleswhere in Ireland. The Druids, hiding in their groves, ostracized from Christian society, ever awaited a return. Their hopes had been dashed by the overthrow of the Norsemen, who however had only time for Almighty Thor. The established

Christian world, torn asunder by the Norsemen and now falling into corruption, would be re-fashioned again by the Normans. The Druids hoped that Christendom might pass away and the Pagan World would arise like a Phoenix and the Dalriada Sea-Kings turn from Christ and once again put faith in Nature.The Druid Cult of the Severed Human head might ride triumphant over the agony of the Cross.

The cutting off of the human head was a Druid habit that persisted well into Christian military practice. Perhaps as Christianity rode triumphant over the scattered remains of Druidism the severed head of one's enemy could still be spied, Druid-fashion, on the dangerous roads in the eleventh and twelfth centuries. The reviving Catholic Church became ever vigilant. Human heads - actual skulls or representatives of them in different art forms, often appeared from crevices in rocks. Cutting off the head of one's enemy during the many cattle raids that must have taken place throughout the long period when Christianity took root, meant that you possessed your enemy's acumen or spirit, and that you gained extra strength thereby. The head of a chieftain or great warrior or soothsayer was a tremendous prize. Perhaps in the deep Glens of Antrim, amongst its cool and mysterious groves on moonlit nights, or in the depth of winter, a handful but subversive minority of Druids would gallop with the heads of their enemies (probably Christian ones) hanging them from their saddles or carrying them aloft on their spears. Perhaps in some cabin in a forest clearing - for the Celts built in logs - heads might be seen nailed to the walls or placed on poles in sanctuaries. The dying Gaelic world became the world of witchcraft and Black Magic; the ancient Druids loomed like fiends.

Old habits died hard: the naked Celtic warrior adorned with helmet, armlets and torgues might spring from the world of Saint Patrick, rule Dalriada, and control the High-Kings at Tara again. The Druid, like the Christian missionary, was a philosopher and he could also turn into a man of violence. However art and architecture were to firmly separate the Pagan Gael from the

Christian Gael. The early Celts built fortified wooden hill forts; by the eleventh century the Norse invasions had added a spur to building in stone, with the erection of defensive round towers. Many of the early monasteries like Iona had been built in stone. After 1169 the Normans built sturdy square-walled castles, a good example of which is Carrickfergus Castle on the banks of Belfast Lough. The great glens of Ireland, during Gaelic independence, had been amply denuded of their timber; now the mountain sides were quarried to help establish the new stone keeps of the Middle Ages, ruled by the armour-clad Normans. It was a total break with the ancient world and a farewell to the Druids. The world of myth and legend is now definitely taken over by the world of Norman bureaucracy and historical facts: it can be safely said that in the north of Ireland the Gaels were loosely united and often in rebellion against the Northern Kingdoms, led by the Uí Neíll Clan by the time of Saint Patrick (432): the Northern Kings ruled from Tara near Dublin as Irish Emperors. The south of Ireland was ruled by the Munster princes, basing themselves at Cashel in the south-west. Both these confederacies had attempted some degree of unity by 1000AD and had looked towards a Scots-Irish cultural sphere, that the Normans became ever aware might encircle and crush the English Monarchy. Myth surrounded the ancestors of these Ui Neill and Eoganachta halves: the north of Ireland, including central Ireland, was known as Leth Cuinn, or Conn's Half; whilst southern Ireland, south of Tara, was known as Leth Moga Nuatha, or Mug's Half. Both these "halves" established "overseas" colonies: Dalriada, in Conn's Half; and parts of Wales, in Mug's Half. Our knowledge of early Ireland comes from such legends as the *Ulster Cycle* - tales memorized in pre-literate times and finally written down some time after the sixth century. Gaelic Civilization, like that of the Incas of South America, was totally illiterate until the arrival of Christianity.

CONQUEST OF THE GAELS

Pope Adrian IV's Bull *Laudabiliter* granted Ireland to the Norman King, Henry II in 1155. Pope Adrian IV was the only Englishman ever to have been Pope. Many believe that *Laudabiliter* was a pious forgery, or an "altered" document, and that the Papacy's true intentions in 1155 were unknown: the only written source of knowledge for the famous (or infamous) Papal Bull is in Giraldus Cambrensis' *Conquest of Ireland*. Like the Spanish conquest of Peru, the Norman advance in Ireland is as incredible as the submission of the Incas: it is the overawing effect of a small number of forces of a technologically advanced civilization, meeting a Gaelic Civilization well in decadence. Ulster was at first left untouched; the Irish bishops and the Nordic Sea-Towns on the east coast of Ireland bowed before Henry II's sword. It was however concerning the struggle for the High-Kingship, involving local feuds in Ulster, that had prompted the Normans, led by Richard de Clare, or Strongbow, to cross from southern Wales. The crossing is described in Irish annals: "The fleet of the Flemings came to Erin, they were ninety heroes dressed in mail, and the Gaels set no store by them". The Normans did not publish *Laudabiliter* in Ireland. The Papacy was aware that Ireland, like other parts of Christendom, was lapsing from the Faith. The See of Armagh was in the grip of family interests: the principle of election should be introduced, and the Gaelic Church should fall under the influence of Canterbury, treading on centuries of tradition. The Bull *Laudabiliter* describes Henry II as "a Catholic prince labouring to extend the borders of the Church and teach the truth of the Christian faith to rule a rude and unlettered people. It is beyond all doubt that Ireland and all other islands which have received the Christian faith belong to Saint Peter and the holy Roman Church". Henry II was "to enter Ireland in order to subdue the people and make them obedient to laws, and that he is willing to pay from every house there one penny to Saint Peter and to keep and preserve the rights of the churches in that land whole and inviolate". Henry II was to be "Lord of Ireland".

On the eve of the Norman invasion, the High-Monarchy of Ireland was in collapse. Dalriada and the other northern kingdoms had been absorbed into Ulster; Murcertach, King of Ulster, became "Emperor of Ireland" in 1162. But Murcertach quarreled with his vassal in eastern Ulster, taking him prisoner and blinding him. The Ulster kings revolted and in turn slew Murcertach, leaving the High-Kingship in doubt and Ireland a prey to foreign rule. Aware that outside intervention might prevent the King of Ulster from dominating Ireland, Dermot MacMurrough, King of Leinster, sailed to Bristol on 1st August 1166. He brought with him his daughter Eva, whom he would offer in marriage to Richard de Clare or Strongbow and Earl of Pembroke, thus securing a Norman soldier-adventurer's right to the Crown of Leinster. The Gaelic Kings acknowledged Dermot's rights. He returned to Leinster in 1167 with a small Norman force, to be followed by the stronger force of six hundred in 1169. In 1171 the Gaelic King of Leinster died, now leaving the kingdom open to its Norman heir. In 1170 Strongbow had landed with a force of one-thousand two hundred, near the Danish town of Waterford, at the tip of south-west Ireland. He brought with him his Gaelic wife, Eva, and warlike intentions.

The Norman chroniclers describe how some of the Irish went naked and unarmed into battle; a good deal of the old pre-Christian Gaelic methods prevailed; perhaps one of the chief reasons why Ireland could not present a united front to the conqueror. Ulster did not take advantage of its geographical position *vis-à-vis* north-west Scotland, forging links in an effort to bring about a dual Scots-Irish kingdom, with perhaps a capital near present-day Larne, Belfast or Glasgow. A Scots-Irish dual monarchy might have penetrated into the south of the larger British island, driving back the French-Norman invaders of England. England always feared invasion from the north. As Ulster joined the rest of Ireland to keep the Normans at bay, the

54

Normans observed that none of the Gaelic soldiers knew of saddles or stirrups and that they fought with an enormous unwieldly axe. The Norman knights wore iron helmets and coats of mail. The great yew bow and arrow was matched against the Irish stone sling. Irish fighters were used to fighting in cattle raids, which often escalated into all-Ireland political feuds for the High-Kingship. It was no longer accepted that Ireland could exist alone as an ancient civilization.Like ancient Greece she must fall under a new Rome, and accept the superiority of Medieval life. At Dublin in 1170 all of Ireland ringed the town, ancient city of the Árd Rís, captured by an alien knight. For them Strongbow was the emissary of an all-mighty lord that ruled the other island with his great broad sword and long bows and warriors clad in mail. Dalriada and the island lordships, including the Isle of Man, sent thirty ships to block Dublin harbour, representatives of a now primitive culture that had made all its contributions. The Gaels and the Vikings had either lost their ferocity or could not marshal it. The Viking commander, John, was a madman and his forces were cut to pieces, himself dying berserk. Strongbow was now urged by his Norman knights to reduce the whole of Ireland; but Strongbow had in mind the might of Henry II. An individual Strongbow victory in Ireland would only be temporary; the Scots-Irish link in the north had to be kept in mind; it would not be long until Henry II himself would cross the Irish Sea to reduce an independent Norman Kingdom: the policy of the Normans was ever to curb the ferocity and independence of their barons.

Henry II had murdered Archbishop Beckett of Canterbury in 1170: Henry used this, and the fact that the Pope considered it Henry II's mission to evangelize the Church, as an excuse to land at Waterford in October 1171 with four-thousand troops. Good works in Ireland might placate Papal wrath. Neither the kings of western Ireland, behind the River Shannon and patrolled by Gaelic fleets, nor the kings of the north, locked behind their mountain and lake barriers, would pay homage to Henry II. The arrival of the King of England signalled an earnest attempt to reduce Ireland and obliterate the realm of the *Ard Ris*, despite the fact that the Gaels were themselves Christians. Here in the west of Europe, Christians were to be treated no better than the pagans and Moslems of the East. Their private kingships were to be treated with contempt and their conversion to Christ and their love of Rome counted as nothing in the face of this latest wave of evangelical Catholicism. Gaelic law did not recognize Strongbow as heir to the Kingdom of Leinster. The Irish looked askance at the Pope's wish that Henry II should be "Lord of Ireland". Henry was cautious: he persued the same policy as in England, to disparage the achievements of the barons and contain their local power, which had the effect of placating the Gaelic kings. The Danes fled from Dublin, backbone of its commercial life, whilst the city was given a charter, linking it with Bristol. At the Synod of Cashel in south-west Ireland, the Gaelic Church was brought into agreement with that of England. Henry II appointed a Justiciar or representative of the King in Ireland. Strongbow took his place under Henry II, and died in 1176.

THE EARLDOM OF ULSTER

Ulster now became the target of the Norman adventurer John de Courcy, who, without permission of Henry II advanced north to attack the Kingdom of Ulidia, which occupied present-day County Down and part of south Antrim. Its capital was Downpatrick, where Saint Patrick was said to be buried. Despite an attempt at northern unity the Gaels were driven back by the knights and the bowmen. These Norman bows were perhaps more ferocious than the Irish axe: six foot long they could penetrate a door four inches deep at a length of a hundred yards; or pierce through a man's leg, armour clad, and pierce the belly of his horse. De Courcy acquired the title of *Princeps Ulidiae* and *Conquestor Ultoniae*, Conqueror of the North. De Courcy was an independent prince and unlike Strongbow he scourned the rule of Henry II. Defences were at first in wood, copying local methods; but large stone keeps soon arose to organize the conquest: Carrickfergus Castle, on the banks of Belfast Lough commanded the whole region: de Courcy started its building in 1180 and today it is one of the finest specimens of a Norman Castle in the British Isles. De Courcy penetrated into Antrim Dalriada, up the Antrim Coast, and into the interior of Ulster, to Lough Neagh. Following him went the Benedictine monks, building their stone monasteries, and introducing European orders, bringing the Gaelic world closer to Rome. Forward came the Holy Cross Fathers, the Knights Templars (the Poor Knights of Christ), the Knights Hospitallers; the Cistercians, the Dominicans, the Franciscans and the Carmelites: European Civilization, under reform of the Roman Church, had at last come into direct grips with the "corrupt" Gaelic Rite. The Kingdom of Ulidia now became a French-Norman plantation. However west of Lough Neagh, across its twelve miles of water, lay the unconquered lands, the lands of the Northern Uí Néill: the Uí Néill had held aloft from Dalriada and had often tried its conquest.

The Kingdom of Oriel, which straddled the present-day border of Northern Ireland and Eire, also fell under the Normans; northern Oriel however was left under Gaelic leadership. Generally speaking de Courcy had succeeded in subduing everything in a line that runs along the County Down Coast, through Belfast and Larne, up the Antrim Coast (where a series of Norman keeps arose), eventually reaching the Giant's Causeway and Coleraine. From Fair Head in Antrim Dalriada he could look across the North Channel to the Mull of Kintyre, and if he strained his eyes fully north he could look across to Scottish Dalriada, still under command of the Kings of Norway: the Norse pirates were busily sacking Glasgow and sending raiding parties down the North Channel, along the coasts of Antrim and Down. The Normans therefore brought their own brand of law. De Courcy could look out to the Kingdom of Scotland, knowing that it was attacking England from the north; but he knew that Henry II rested content that it had never succeeded in overrunning the Hebrides and Argyll, as yet.

Across Lough Neagh, abounding in salmon and eels, the Gaels were under the strong Uí Néill leadership: here lay the unsubdued Kingdom of Aileach; beyond this, in the wild lands of Donegal, lay the Kingdom of the O'Donnells. The O'Neills and the O'Donnells were determined never to submit to the Normans: they, together with the tribes of Fermanagh, centred around its expanse of lakes, were nonplussed at the arrival of such advanced warriors. Civilized Christian and barbaric Christian confronted. The Crown feared the power of de Courcy, who ruled from Dundrum in County Down: fearful of his power de Courcy was taken prisoner and died in his native France in 1219. Hugh de Lacy was created Norman "Earl of Ulster", which in theory meant that he claimed lordship over the Kingdom of Aileach and the other Gaelic kingdoms of Ulster; his effective jurisdiction was over only parts of Antrim and Down; but again the new King of England, King John, feared the power of this all-powerful baron, as he feared the power of the other barons, both the Gaelic and Norman in Ireland, and the Anglo-Saxon and Norman barons of England. There was a short siege at Carrickfergus; John, landing in Ireland himself, marched north. De Lacy fled, and Ulster fell into King John's hands whilst Richard Coeur de Lion was campaigning and colonizing in the Holy Land. Meanwhile the O'Neills and the O'Donnells were setting aside ancient feuds and uniting in the face of the inevitable Norman assault from across Lough Neagh; it would not be long before the great armoured warriors, confronting these Gaelic "Red Indians", would penetrate the forests of the west, into present-day Fermanagh and Tyrone, and to Derry, to advance across the Foyle estuary and Lough Swilly and into the rocky strongholds of the O'Donnells themselves. At a battle near Portrush in Antrim Dalriada the western Gaels of Ulster established a vague unity that lasted until 1603, when the Gaelic earls submitted to England. The appearance of King John in Ireland further established Norman power: he returned to England in August 1210;but the arrogant barons were able to extort *Magna Carta* from him in 1215.

The Normans advanced into the Kingdom of Connaught in 1235: from here they would try to penetrate to Upper and Lower Lough Erne from their bases on the River Shannon, which runs obliquely through central Ireland. From Connaught they could attack the lands of the O'Donnells from Fermanagh. After a temporary success the O'Donnells won back their territory at the Battle of Credan in 1257. The O'Neills of Tyrone feared this sudden accession of O'Donnell strength, having repulsed the conqueror; the O'Neills were beaten by the ambitious O'Donnells on the banks of the River Swilly. The troubled state of the North gave the men of the Isles and Argyll yet another chance to send raiding parties. Once again they came in their longships, now with Medieval trappings. They were the gallowglasses, half Scots and half Viking, with their great axes, fixed on shafts longer than a man's body. The O'Donnells, of earlier Scottish origins, and backed by the gallowglasses, became overlords of Tyrconnell, Sligo and Fermanagh, in a kingdom that straddles present-day Donegal and Northern Ireland. The Irish now had effective military strength to oppose the Normans: the gallowglasses were young Hebridean men of fine physic, clad in armour themselves. The gallowglasses were merceneries not only to the Ulster chieftains, but penetrated far into southern Ireland along the winding rivers, particulary the Shannon, to hack out kingdoms of their own. They provided a stimulus to the declining Gaelic Civilization. They brought methods that might drive back the Normans, and regain political independence for Ulster and the other kingdoms of Ireland. There was a chance that the O'Neills might obtain the High-Kingship; but this led to internal feuds in Ulster in 1260: the dream of a united Ireland, either ruled from the north or from the south was departing. It was up to Scotland, under the Bruce leadership, to harken after the Gaelic dream of a Scots-Irish dual monarchy. A Scots-Irish dual monarchy might establish the idea that there was no difference between a Scotsman and an Irishman, and that all were Gaels; that all should unite against the Normans, the conquerors of both Gaels and Anglo-Saxons. The intervention of the men of the Isles led to the hope in 1263 that King Haakon of Norway might assist the Irish High-Kingship. Haakon still collected tribute from the Hebrides; but by now the Kings of Scotland were determined to master the independent-minded Islesmen. But the Sea-King of Norway, King Haakon, was defeated at Largs by Alexander III.

Norman law (or English law as it was becoming) as the Anglo-Saxons cleverly absorbed the conquerors, regarded all Irishmen as serfs or villeins (*Hibernicus*). English law was only effective where the Anglo-Normans ruled; elsewhere, especially in Ulster west of Lough Neagh and the River Bann, Gaelic law prevailed. But the sophisticated Norman lords could be as quarrelsome as Gaelic chieftains: the power of the Norman Monarchy declined under the assault of the barons, who fought over land in a game of power politics; whilst the Irish, as usual, fought over land and cattle and only turned to politics if either the north or the south resumed the struggle for the High-Kingship; or if they united against the conqueror. Two thirds of Ireland came under Anglo-Norman law: Ireland was divided into shires or counties, each shire having its Sheriff and Shire-Court. The language of Parliament was French and it assumed that it legislated for the whole island. Parliament (*Parlement*) legislated however only effectively for the Norman townships: these were taking the place of the Danish-ruled seaports. Documentary records were kept in regard to the government of Ireland; but these were destroyed when the Public Record Office in Dublin was burnt down in the political upheavals of 1922, on the eve of England relinquishing control over twenty six of the Irish counties. By the late thirteenth and early fourteenth centuries the Norman lordship was at its height. The Monarchy in England was starting to become distinctly English as Anglo-Norman barons arose: they would eventually, in the fifteenth century, struggle to

60

take the place of the Norman House of Plantagenet in favour of a Yorkist, Lancastrian or Tudor King.

In Ulster, as elsewhere in Ireland, the Normans were becoming as Irish as the Irish. Gaelic Civilization was of course not uninfluenced by the Normans, and the Irish race, a mixture of cultures, started to emerge. The Anglo-Norman Earls of Ulster extended the theoretical power of their Earldom beyond Lough Neagh and the River Bann to the borders of Donegal: central Ulster, domain of the great O'Neills, became a feudal vassal to the foreigners, but enjoyed practical independence. Many of the Anglo-Normans identified with the Gaels and won a measure of confidence from them; they were however regarded by the Dublin Parliament as "degenerate English". The French-speaking English magnate of the fourteenth century was aghast at the degenerate English habit of wearing long hair in the Irish fashion, known as *coolun*. Laws were passed forbidding the wearing of long hair and following other Irish traditions. The Parliament of 1310 passed an act stipulating that "no mere Irishman shall be received into a religious order among the English in the land of peace". A "mere Irishman" of course was a "degenerate Englishman", a "whiteman" that lorded it over and identified with the natives. "The land of peace" was that part of Ireland under Anglo-Norman rule. The "mere Irish" were the *Merus Hibernicus*, men accepting Gaelic law rather than English law; but it was a Gaelic law that was also "accepting" a lot of Anglo-Norman Civilization, when convenience arose, despite the ancient traditions of the Northern Uí Néill lords. However feelings about treating fellow Anglo-Normans as outcasts was reviled by the English Archbishop of Armagh, who got the act revoked by an appeal to the King. The help of the Anglo-Irish and Gaelic Ulstermen was needed in England's Scottish wars. The forty to fifty foot long Medieval ship, with platform stern and castle bow, and colourful square sail, carried men-at-arms across the North Channel. But the Anglo-Norman Earl of Ulster was the father-in-law of Robert Bruce, the struggling King of Scotland and enemy of England; so the campaigns of Ulstermen in Scotland were at best to be half-hearted, having a dual allegiance. The dream of a Scots-Irish dual Monarchy became a possibility once again.

THE BRUCE INVASION

Alexander III, who had driven the King of Norway out of the Scottish Islands, died in 1286: he had no children; so the King of Norway's daughter, Alexander's grandchild, became heir to the Scottish throne. Edward I, King of England, in an effort to win Scotland peacefully, suggested that Margaret should marry his - Edward's - son. A treaty stipulated that southern Scotland should be garrisoned with English troops. At this the Scots nobility rose up. However Margaret died in the Orkney Islands on her way from Norway. Amongst the claimants now to the Scottish throne was the Anglo-Norman lord, Robert de Brus. He had fought in Edward I's armies, and he had estates in England. However Robert de Brus's rival, Balliol, won the Crown of Scotland: Edward I himself thought that Balliol would be a more amenable character and would truckle to England's will. But Balliol unexpectedly concluded an alliance with France and prepared to invade northern England. The southern Scots, owning land in England, paid homage to Edward I as he advanced to counter Balliol. Amongst Edward's venerators was Robert de Brus, whose lands were now seized by the Scots King. Balliol however was defeated by Edward I and lodged in the Tower of London. Edinburgh, Stirling, Perth and Elgin fell to the English. In 1296 the King of England carried off from Scotland to London the ancient Crowning Stone of the Scottish Kings, which Fergus of Antrim Dalriada had brought from Ulster thirty generations ago.

Robert de Brus's son, Robert Bruce, accepting all the Anglo-Norman traditions, continued his father's struggle for the throne:

62

early on, Robert Bruce got involved in a personal dispute with one of his rivals, stabbing him to death in the Greyfriars Kirk at Dumfries. However one of Robert's brothers, Edward Bruce, did not desert him, despite Robert's excommunication by the Church. Help would be forthcoming from Ulster and the foundations for the invasion of Ireland would be laid as Robert Bruce had himself crowned King of Scots in 1306. England soon dealt with the forces of the Bruce. Robert Bruce escaped after the Battle of Methven in 1306, and fled north to the Hebrides and to the King of Norway, leading a roaming life; then sneaking south down the island lordships, to Rathlin Island: Rathlin Island lies only five miles off the coast of Antrim Dalriada. It is said that Scotland's future King hid in a sandstone cave at the south-west corner of the island: he would have looked out to the mountain peak of the Mull of Kintyre, only twelve miles distant, regarding Rathlin as part of Scotland. In his anxious moments, thinking all was lost, and that his brother Edward might side with England to save his own neck, he saw a gigantic spider groping in the sandstone. Its devilish eyes are said to have looked at Robert Bruce in the darkness. The life Bruce was leading soon determined him to return to mainland Scotland, to arouse the Highland lords. The death of Edward I, King of England in 1307, proved to be a turning point. The King of France secretly recognized Robert as King of Scots, whilst the Church in Scotland came out on his side, despite his continuing excommunication by the Pope. On 24 June 1314 Robert Bruce's army, comprised of the nobles of Scotland, with Irish mercenaries, defeated the new English King Edward II at the Battle of Bannockburn. Bruce had been outnumbered three to one; but the waterlogged meadows were said to have proved the downfall of the superior English numbers. Now Robert invaded England as the English had invaded Scotland; in 1316 he carried the war into Ireland, in an effort to corner England and to eventually lay the foundations of Scottish domination of the whole British Isles. In 1316 Robert Bruce (Robert I) bestowed the Crown of Ireland upon his brother Edward. The ancient idea of the Gaelic dual monarchy had a chance of triumphing at last. In 1322 Edward II of England tried to combat Scotland, but was chased back into Yorkshire, losing his personal baggage. The Pope now annuled Bruce's excommunication against the wishes of England. Court intrigue now set Edward III on the throne of England in 1327. In 1328 England recognized Robert Bruce as King of Scotland. A year later Bruce died, having used the title of *Rex Scottorum* or Emperor of the Scots, claiming rule over Scotland and Ireland. He followed in the footsteps of Brian Boru, the Irish High-King and Irish Gael. England saw the menace of a Scots-Irish Empire to the north that would soon raid England and neutralize her monarchy. The Normans may have had in mind the *Scotti* raiders that ravaged the west coast of England when the Romans withdrew in the fifth century. It had been Niall of the Nine Hostages who had sent his *Scotti* raiders from Ulster.

However Robert's attempts to include Ireland in the *Rex Scottorum* were regarded by the Irish as they had regarded Norman attempts at colonization. The devastations of his brother Edward's campaign left a permanent mark upon Scots-Irish relations, politically dividing the Gaelic race. On 25 May 1315 Edward Bruce sailed across the North Channel in his flimsy medieval ships, landing at Olderfleet (Larne) in south-eastern Antrim. It is said to have been the biggest invading force ever landed on Irish soil, an army of six thousand clad in mail, and game for the Anglo-Normans, hated now by the Irish Church, the Gaelic lords and by the Scots descended lords of Antrim. The Norman Earl of Ulster was defeated at Connor, and Robert Bruce moved south, in victory after victory, adding a spur to a general Gaelic resurgence. Unity of the north and south would again be established and the Normans driven out. Edward Bruce would be King of Ireland, and vassal to his brother Robert, *Rex Scottorum*. All the north, except the great stronghold of Carrickfergus Castle on the banks of present-day Belfast Lough (then known as Knockfergus Bay) was in his hands; but it was near Dundalk, geographically in the north of Ireland, that Edward Bruce was

64

proclaimed "King of Erin".

Now Bruce marched westwards, taking the Kingdom of Connaught; at last returning north to turn his attention to Carrickfergus Castle. His brother Robert Bruce crossed from Scotland to join in the abortive siege. Meanwhile the Norman Earl of Ulster, a wandering vagabond throughout Ireland, sought refuge in Dublin. He organized its defences, and successfully withstood the Bruce siege, forcing them back north. Already the *Rex Scottorum* was laying the foundations of his own defeat in Ireland. He frightened the Gaelic lords by the success of his campaigns against the demoralized Normans, devastating their domain, waging general rapine, with all the immoralities and vices that attend an invading force.The Normans, at the end of their tether, gave the Irish equality before the law, and played upon their natural fear of being dominated by a colonial Scotland, perhaps worse than a colonial England. It had been said before that the Normans regarded killing Irishmen as they would have regarded killing dogs.They marshalled their forces to drive out the Bruce. Robert Bruce was slain by a colonial force near Dundalk on 14 October 1318. The Scots retreated north, running for the ships, to return to help consolidate Scotland against fresh Norman assaults from the north of England. The dream of the Empire of the Gaels had been dashed; for political and even racial differences had appeared amongst the Scots and Irish: the North Channel was starting to divide them; and even the Scots of Antrim, ancient Dalriada, had veered towards the Irish; whilst Scotland had formed an independent Kingdom of her own with Continental alliances. Gaelic Ireland, the island of the warring Goidels, was now again subjected to Norman colonial rule and Ulster bowed before a fresh succession of overlords. However the traditional Norman cruelty had gone; perhaps they had learnt something from the Anglo-Saxons, for the Normans granted *Magna Carta* to Ireland and English liberty to some of the Irish chiefs. The Scots devastations had done irreparable damage to the Anglo-Norman Lordship. The Gaelicized Norman lords, like the

Earl of Ulster, had looked to the power of England to reinforce their local principalities; whilst their assuming of local customs had sometimes endeared them to the Irish. It seemed better to accept a Gaelicized Norman, half alien to the English Monarchy, than a domineering Scot; a Norman tyrant was better than a rising arrogant Scots one. The native annals record that Edward Bruce was "the destroyer of Ireland in general, both of the English and the Gael" and that "there was not done from the beginning of the world a better deed for the men of Erin than that deed, for theft, famine, and destruction of men occured throughout Erin for the space, of three years and a half, and the people used actually to eat one another thoughout the island". The effect of the Scots campaign on Scots-Irish relations could be likened to the effect of the Great Famine of 1845-47 on Anglo-Irish relations. 1315-1327 confirmed Irish antipathy towards Scotland; whilst 1845-47 confirmed Irish antipathy to England.The already existing Scots population in Ireland, especially in north-eastern Ulster was to suffer as a consequence and become increasingly isolated.

THE BLACK DEATH

The Black Death came in 1348: it is reckoned to have wiped out one third of Ireland's population. The population of Ireland was about one million. Word of the plague had spread to European seaports by 1346, that a supernatural evil had befallen the East. It was thought that the plague might not spread into Europe. Ireland, on the fringe of Europe, seemed to be safe from the horror; and even if it spread to England, the Irish Sea and the North Channel would prove an insuperable obstacle. As often as not the sea links between England and Dublin and between Antrim and the north-west of Scotland proved to be a convenient route rather than the obstacle in the spread of this malignancy. It was a plague of unparalled fury and consumed Scots, Irish,

Anglo-Saxon and Norman alike, holding no distinction between Christian or Druid, infecting the dead as well as the living. It was heard at Carrickfergus and Armagh, and in Dublin, that "India was depopulated, Tartary, Mesopotamia, Syria, Armenia were covered with dead bodies; the Kurds fled in vain to the mountains. In Caramania and Caesarea none were left alive ..." Eighty-five thousand were said to be dead in the Crimea alone.

It is thought that the Black Death came to Ireland through the shipping links, arriving in England with sailors from the East and the Mediterranean. Along with the spices of the Orient and rich jewels to adorn and beautify the Anglo-Norman and Gaelic body, travelled a horror that would scar and disfigure the wealthy, and then spread amongst the poor. Anti-Christ had come, to punish the immoralities of the lascivious Medieval mind. The quarrels of the north and the south of Ireland, the growing enmity between Scots and Irish and the universal hatred of the Normans, was suddenly interrupted by the appearance of boils and blisters on the body. These could grow to the size of an apple. The infection would first be seen in the groin or under an armpit. It would then spread furiously throughout the system, until the whole body was covered in a black puss. Sometimes a miracle would happen and the priest would exclaim that God had brought about recovery; or villages and towns would have faith that the bubonic plague was being chased away by the power of the Church. The victim in his death throes would cough blood and his breathing would become an hysterical effort. Mortality generally lasted several months. The last time the plague had travelled west was in 664, a halocaust the medieval mind thought could never recur; it had travelled west at the time of the extension of the Gaelic Church. The Medieval *Pasteurella Pestis* found its home in the blood stream of animals or in the stomach of fleas; then rodents would be infected. The most deadly and far travelling of these rodents was the *rattus rattus* or Black Rat that would migrate in Central Asia in response to famine and floods. Infected rats could reach Europe in the boats of returning Crusaders;

however the flea itself was an equally independent source for infecting Man. The effects on the brain could be devastating before death, simulating the behaviour of the mad: the Christian might lose his faith and harken after the Druids; or an unbeliever might become religious as he faced a horrible death.The agonizing boils on the body, in a Medieval world of violence like Ireland, could make contenders even more violent and commit even greater outrages - or alternatively interrupt the course of confrontation.

Ireland was not to be immune from the Black Death for long: it probably came through Bristol to Dublin in 1348, travelling north along the great north-south highway, that ended at Dunseverick on the cold but healthy shores of the Antrim Coast. On the other hand it could have come directly, and at the same time, from Brittany via the Celtic Sea, infecting the warmer south west of Ireland, and then travelling north to infect Dublin and Ulster. John Clyn, of the Order of the Friars Minor and of the Convent of Kilkenny wrote that "... in the months of September and October, bishops, prelates, priests, friars, noblemen and others, women as well as men, came in great numbers from every part of Ireland to the pilgrimage centre of that Molyngis (on the River Burrow). So great were their numbers that on many days it was possible to see thousands of people flocking there; some through devotion but others, the majority, through fear of the plague, which then was very prevalent. It began near Dublin at Howth and at Drogheda. These cities were almost entirely destroyed and emptied of inhabitants so that Dublin alone, between the beginning of August and Christmas, fourteen-thousand people died". However in 1349 Richard Fitzralph of Armagh, visiting the Pope at Avignon, declared that the plague had destroyed two thirds of England, whilst Scotland and Ireland had largely escaped.There is a good deal of confusion about how badly the plague hit Ireland; but modern research has come down in favour of John Clyn's record, and not that of Armagh. Even while the Archbishop of Armagh was making his way to Avignon (the Medieval castle refuge of the Popes as captives of the French Kings), a journey which would have taken him about three weeks, the plague was spreading into the Irish midlands and into the west. The *Annals of Connaught* declare that "A great plague ... in all Ireland this year. Matha, son of Cathal O'Ruaire died of the plague. The earl's grandson died. Risdered O'Raigillig, King of East Brefni died". The friaries, backbone of the Medieval Church in Ireland, were devastated and the economic prosperity that everywhere characterized this period of the High Middle Ages - despite the Bruce Wars - was shattered: the price of provisions escalated. The Normans and the Norman-Irish were almost wiped out, since they were more easily infected, using the products of the seaports more than the indigenous Gaelic population.

The Black Death, following closely on the Bruce invasion, permanently weakened Anglo-Norman rule throughout Ireland. Ulster developed her traditional independent position. However the Scots in Ireland or the newly established Scots Kingdom could gain no capital out of the plague's effects. It was said that the Scots were delighted when they heard of the fate of the English, amassing forces at the Scots border in preparation to invade, unaware that they would be victims themselves. They laughed and shrieked at the thousands dying in Northumberland and Durham; but it was their last laugh: "... the fearful mortality fell upon them and the Scots were scattered by sudden and savage death so that, within a short period, some five thousand died". However the Scots remarked that the Black Death attacked" ... the meaner sort and common people; - seldom the magnates". This was true also of England: only in Ireland did the poorer classes fare better than the magnates, perhaps because of their remoteness and reluctance to have intercourse with the Anglo-Norman world. The destruction of between one third and one half of Ireland's population would bring about new economic alignments, even though the feudal economic system had been in the process of change and development anyway. As in England and everywhere in Europe the institution of serfdom was ruined. Fewer peasants meant a chronic labour shortage. Landlords who no longer had serfs enough to till the open fields were inevitably tempted to offer wages: this of course would largely affect the English-ruled areas of the eastern seaboard; but the Gaelic economy suffered likewise. England up till 1348 had been over-populated, which helped to account for her expansion into Wales, Scotland, and of course into Ireland; halving of the English population put a break upon English expansion, making her more inclined to consolidate her internal political fabric; whilst the weakening of the Anglo-Norman lordship gave a chance for a Gaelic recovery: this would give the north-south struggle a new lease of life. Nor could the effects upon the Church be ignored. As the plague petered out in 1405, a fresh spate of friar building and restoration took place. The central authority of the Papacy was weakening, now that the Popes had moved to Avignon in 1305, returning to Rome in 1403. A few thinkers were starting to talk about the Bible and to hold private interpretations as the Catholic Church fell into one of its many decadences: in one hundred and fifty years Martin Luther would be born. The Archdiocese of Armagh was divided and the Archbishop would not dare live in the Cathedral City. The clergy started to look like laymen, with long hair and moustaches: they were becoming "degenerate Englishmen", often living openly with women. Lack of celibacy meant the problem of heirs, so that it was not unusual for members of a Catholic bishop's "family" to regard ecclesiastical property as a family possession. This also held true of the monasteries.

The shock of the "economic chaos, social unrest, high prices, profiteering, depravation of morals, lack of production, industrial idolence, frenetic gaiety, wild expenditure, luxury, debauchery, social and religious hysteria, greed, avarice, maladministration, decay of manners" would lead to inevitable recovery, to renaissance and reformation. The period 1350 - 1600 ended in England changing her religion. Catholic Ireland would prefer her Catholic allegiance, and struggled with the new English

Protestant system, whilst the Scots entrenched themselves in the north. The Lordship of the Isles, linked to the Lords of Antrim, was now formally allied with England to combat the menace of Scotland by a series of treaties in 1392, 1394 and 1398. They were signed as between two sovereign states.

THE GAELIC REVIVAL

It was left to the O'Neills of Tyrone, who ruled the lands equivalent to present-day counties Londonderry, Armagh and Tyrone, to carry the torch of Gaelic Ulster. Ulster took part in the Gaelic revival that was happening everywhere in Ireland as a result of the Norman decline.The Normans still assumed that they held ultimate sway: Donal O'Neill was banished into the wilds of Tyrone as the Norman "Red Earl" of Ulster was restored. When the "Red Earl" died in 1326 his grandson, William "Donn" ("the Brown Earl") succeeded him. Family feud rent Norman Ulster apart as much as Gaelic Ulster: the "Brown Earl" was murdered at the "Ford of Carrickfergus" on 6 June 1333: this had considerable long term effects; for although Gaelic Ulster and Gaelic Ireland were gathering strength, the murder of a semi-independent Norman Earl, who veered towards Gaelic tradition and treated the King of England as an Irishman would, meant that the Earldom of Ulster fell into Royal hands. Lionel, Duke of Clarence, became Earl of Ulster and the greatest feudal lord in Ireland. He was however an absentee. The local Ulster chieftains rose up in the face of Anglo-Norman weakness, reducing the effectiveness of the Earldom to the present-day coasts of Antrim and Down: here resided the Norman-Irish vassals of the Earldom: the real Gaels were secure in their mountain strongholds of the Antrim Hills and Mourne Mountains, in the Sperrin Mountains of central Ulster, and in Donegal, ready for rebellion. In petty battle after petty battle the Gaelic chieftains had won back their lost

71

territories from the Anglo-Normans, pushing them back into their castles on the eastern coast. The O'Neills, at the head of the northern tradition, and hacking out an independent north, advanced towards Belfast. Hugh-Boy O'Neill, with gallowglass mercenaries, ejected the Normans from northern Antrim, having advanced across the River Bann. The River Bann divides Ulster into two: the Gaelic west of Ulster and the Scots-Gaelic east of Ulster (Antrim and Down). The Glens of Antrim were cleared of real Norman and "degenerate English" alike. The O'Neill passed by Belfast on his way into the Ards Peninsula, and after several years the great Norman Savage family was subdued. As a later Irish Attorney-General wrote: "So about the thirtieth year of King Edward the Third ... the Savages were utterly driven out of the Great Ardes into a little nook of land near the river of Strangford, where they now possess a little territory called the Little Ards; and their greater patrimony took the name of the Upper Clan Hugh Boy O'Neill, who became invaders thereof".

The Normans had built a castle at the strategic ford of Belfast: this linked their conquered territories in Antrim and Down; but its history may be traced back to the Vikings. Belfast itself means "the mouth of, or approach to, the sand bank". At low tide it was possible to wade across Belfast Lough to the County Down Coast, using the ford at Belfast. The Norman Castle is said to date from the thirteenth century, standing in the present-day Castle Place and Castle Lane region: Belfast stood at the foot of the great Cave Hill, which dominates the modern city. It is said that the Cave Hill, whose caves were inhabited in Stone Age times, may have been used as a lookout spot in a later age for Viking invaders sailing up Belfast Lough. However throughout the Norman Lordship, Carrickfergus Castle was the main supply depot. When Hugh-Boy O'Neill overran Antrim and Down, the Castle of Belfast passed into Gaelic hands. Only on the coast did the original Normans survive in reduced numbers: the Savages of the Ards; Byset, Lord of the Glens of Antrim and the Mandevilles of "the Route" in North Antrim (the ancient Dalriada Kingdom

72

that still of course had links with the Highlands and Islands). The period of Gaelic resurgence is noted for the submergence of Norman families into the Ulster fabric; thus the Mandevilles of "the Route" became the Gaelic MacQuillans. English efforts to recover the Earldom were disparged by the Gaelicized Normans who wrote that the Justiciar sent "as an invader of the rights of the clerics and of the lay, rich and poor, a robber of goods under the colour of the good, the defrauder of the many, never observing the law of the Church nor that of the State, inflicting many evils on the native-born, the poor only excepted, in which things he was led by the council of his wife". By the time of the Black Death in 1348 the Anglo-Normans had become permanently estranged from the Crown. They persued their own social and economic policies, keeping in mind the Gaelic law.This was a process that the Black Death, famines and the Bruce Invasion was to hasten. An English edict in 1361 stated that "no pure-blooded Irishman of the Irish nation shall be made mayor, bailiff, or officer of any place subject to the King or hold a canonry or living among the English; yet at the request of Irish clerics living among the English we ordain that such Irishmen, of whose loyalty our judges are assured, shall not be molested".

The Normans considered that the best means of defending their Irish Lordship was to attack Irish institutions by means of statute and law. The Irish Parliament met at Kilkenny in 1366, in south-east Ireland, to pass the famous "Statutes of Kilkenny"; in modern terms this could be castigated as a "racialist" document that forever divided the Gael from the Englishman and cemented racial antipathy. The language was Norman-French, and the Statutes were passed at the instigation of Lionel, Duke of Clarence, who had become heir to the Ulster Earldom: the Statutes of Kilkenny were to remain in force well into the Tudor and Reformation period: " ... now many English of the said land (Ireland) forsaking the English language, fashion, mode of riding, laws and usages, live and govern themselves according to the manners, fashion, and language of the Irish enemies, and have also made divers marriages and alliances between themselves and the Irish enemies aforesaid; whereby the said land the liege people thereof, the English language, the allegiance due to our lord the King, and the English laws there, are put in subjection and decayed". For all those who would contravene the laws, the three archbishops and five bishops present amongst the other delegates at Kilkenny Castle, published a sentence of excommunication. The main effect of the Statutes was to preserve the eastern English-speaking areas, and to keep the Gaelic "wild west" of Ireland, resurgent now in Ulster, at bay. It was a piece of Norman regulation at the height of decadence. The Anglo-Normans had "become more Irish than the Irish themselves"; real "degenerate Englishmen". The Church was prohibited from receiving an Irishman within its community: thus the brave Gaels that had evangelized Scotland and the north of England, and established a Gaelic Church, were excluded from the material community of Christ by the Normans, acting under the Roman tradition. Moreover another clause forbade "the games which men call hurlings with great clubs at ball upon the ground, from which great evils and maims have arised to the weakening and defence of the said land". The Statutes were impossible to enforce: just as the Normans in England became English, so the Normans in Ireland became Irish. Anglicized Normans therefore looked down upon and wished to ostracize Norman-Irishmen and the Gaelic Irish alike. Although the Statutes of Kilkenny tried to obliterate the difference between Englishmen born in England and Englishmen born in Ireland; in social and cultural terms a difference always persisted: one was Irish and the other an Englishman. The English born in Ireland, or Anglo-Irish, were regarded as potential rebels, and more dangerous because of their local independence and wealth than the native Gaels. The Crown always relied upon Englishmen born in England to uphold its authority in the shrinking Irish Lordship. The influence of Norman upon Irishman worked both ways; for as we have seen, the Irish soon copied French methods of warfare: they used seals and made

74

treaties in the continental manner, but held fast to the Gaelic tongue. They scorned hereditary succession by primogeniture: when a ruler died a successor was elected from amongst "the family". The widening cultural divide was to bring to a head the struggle between the Gaelic and English law by the time of the Reformation in the sixteenth century.

THE LORD OF THE NORTH

In 1394 King Richard II of England landed at Waterford in the south of Ireland with thirty-thousand archers and four thousand men-at-arms. He had come to subdue the colourful chieftains, who sought to restore the realm of the *Ard Rís* Norman power was falling apart not only in Ireland, but in England. Richard II had already written from England to the Great O'Neill of Tyrone that he "promised to do justice to everyman". Niall More O'Neill had made his way south to the Norman town of Drogheda, where he submitted on 16 March in the name of his father. With the exception of a few of his more warlike vassals and the pirate princes of Connaught, he promised to surrender all lands to the Crown (receiving them back from the King) and to come to parliaments and councils when summoned. From this date the Gaelic chiefs dropped the title of "King" in their titles. The O'Neills became known by their clan, ruling a specified area; it was up to Shane O'Neill, enemy of Elizabeth I, to revive the Ulster Kingship, and to help start another Gaelic resurgence, which took place during times of England's lack of authority over Ireland. O'Neill and the other chieftains made their homage in Gaelic, whilst the Norman-Irish took theirs in French or English. O'Neill made no attempt to hand over English lands, which the Crown claimed he had usurped. English law recognized O'Neill's Irish territories. However "the great submission" was never enacted by the Dublin Parliament. The twenty-five year old Roger Mortimer, heir to the childless Richard II, was left to recover

75

Ulster; he was slain wearing the light linen dress of an Irish chieftain. Richard again landed at Waterford on 1 June 1399, enraged at Roger Mortimer's death; but the Irish defied the King with impunity. O'Neill sat back in the north as the colourful Art MacMurrough Kavanagh openly met Richard in some wild glen in his Kingdom of Leinster, to tell the Plantagenet that "I am rightful King of Ireland and it is unjust to deprive me of what is my land by conquest". Dynastic feud in England, let alone dynastic struggles in Ireland, hastened Richard's return, to face deposition and death. The last of the Norman Kings of England had given way to the House of Lancaster and Henry IV, and to the English race.

In 1397 a Spanish pilgrim, Count Perilhos, set out to visit Lough Derg in Donegal, part of the northern tribal confederacy. The English gave him ample warnings about the perils of probing deep into native territory and the barbarities that might befall the civilized. Lough Derg was one of Saint Patrick's missionary spots, and it was then, as it is now, one of the most celebrated places in Christendom. There was a cave situated on a tiny island in the Red Lake that was said to lead to the depths of Hell. Men were said to have gone in and experienced terrible horrors and had come out madmen. The cave, the Entrance to Hell, was demolished in 1497 on the authority of Pope Alexander VI. Count Perilhos, however, was determined to face the dangers of Ulster and to go on a pilgrimage. To go on pilgrimage was a favourite Medieval habit, either to the Holy Land or other famous European places like Rome or Canterbury. The Archbishop of Armagh gave the Count a bodyguard; but the bodyguards fled when faced with probing into the domain of the Great O'Neill of the North. The Count must have been convinced that O'Neill was not as fierce or as unlearned as the English, warring amongst themselves, had made out. The Great O'Neill treated him well - perhaps because he was a Spaniard - and they spent Christmas together. Count Perilhos described how the O'Neill lords were clad in knee length tunics, on top of which they wore great hooded cloaks, protecting them from

76

the snow and wild rain of the north. At meal times the Great O'Neill wiped his mouth with delicately cut grass; whilst Count Perilhos was presented with "two little cakes as thin as wafers, and they bent like raw dough and they were oats and earth, as black as coals, although they were very tasty". As for the subjects of the Great O'Neill, living off beef and milk, they "go as they can, ill-clothed, but the principal of them wear cloaks of woollen plush; and they show all the shameful parts, the women as well as the men". The lifestyle of the O'Neills was not to change substantially in the next two hundred years. Locked behind the fastness of dark green mountains and glens, and in the cold wintry sunsets of the north, the struggle to preserve Gaelic Civilization took root in the souls of these barbarians, as the English and contemporary travellers called them: they existed in a twilight world: it had been given a temporary, but extended life, as England fell into dynastic feud, but which would be inevitably challenged by England in a final and crushing defeat.

Part Three

IRISH AND ENGLISH

GAELIC AND ENGLISH LAW

Conn O'Neill had been made Earl of Tyrone by Henry VIII in 1542: the Gaelic earls of Ulster, like their southern counterparts, and like the Anglo-Irish Earls of Kildare (representatives of the Crown in Ireland), were content with local powers, whilst doing homage to the English Crown. By now the British Isles was taking on a more familiar political form. The Norman strain in the English ruling classes had almost died out, and the Tudors had ascended the throne in 1485 after the wars between the Houses of Lancaster and York. The Scots were still troublesome, and laws had been brought into force stopping the Scots of the Isles crossing into Ulster and stirring up trouble. The basic Scottish political unit had taken form. Later on Elizabeth I rejoiced that Scotland would become infected with Protestantism, drawing the Crowns of England and Scotland together at a future date: this would alienate Ireland, which preferred its Papal allegiance. The English had forsaken their French manners, whilst the Scots lords spoke in English; both lived on the verge of the Age of Nationalism. The Gaelic world, of course, had been rent asunder by the famine, pestilence and the Bruce invasion of the late Middle Ages: the idea of a dual Gaelic Monarchy, embracing Scotland and Ireland, with Continental alliances, to combat the power of England, was now shattered. The petty kingdoms of Ireland, with the Scottish north-east of Ulster, were starting to adopt English manners. The great O'Neills of the North, like the great Desmonds of the south-west, lived in the shadow of the real Gaelic world; this had said its last farewell under the Norman conquest. Just as the English became Anglo-Norman, so the Irish became Irish-Norman: out of this process the English nation emerged by the time of the Tudors; whilst the tribal system in Ireland was breaking down. The great O'Neill had accepted an English title - Earl of Tyrone - instead of insisting upon keeping his Gaelic title, "The O'Neill". The Gaelic earls showed diplomacy: refusal to comply with the ever encroaching English would have meant a premature confrontation with the Crown, and certain extinction without foreign help. Despite the south-west of Ireland's frequent intercourse with Spain and France, help was far off, as yet, from that direction; whilst in the north the Scots were concentrating on consolidating their own Monarchy: the Lordship of the Isles was suppressed in 1499, bringing the Scots Gaelic clans within the orbit of Edinburgh Castle, and united in the face of England: England had tried to maintain the Lordship as an independent foreign power to limit the power of the Scots Monarchy.

When Elizabeth I came to the throne in 1558, the Reformation and Protestantism were in full swing. England had plenty of enemies: the restlessness of the Ulster chieftains, perhaps more than the Desmond rebellion that started in 1569 in the south-west, was a real threat. Shane O'Neill started his career as the outcast son of Conn O'Neill, for Conn's illigitimate son, Matthew, was to inherit the English-bestowed title of Earl of Tyrone. Shane O'Neill protested to Elizabeth that he himself was Conn's legitimate son, implying that Conn O'Neill had no business accepting an English title when a Gaelic one was better. He demanded that he, Shane O'Neill, should be Conn O'Neill's rightful heir; and that Shane O'Neill, a real Gael of the north, should adopt the title of "The O'Neill". Shane, of course, was aware that his father, Conn, was no soft-hearted semi-English gentleman: Conn O'Neill had aspired to the throne of Ireland in 1539, when he and the earls of the south had tried to invade the Dublin Pale: Conn was to have been crowned King of Ireland at Tara, with dreams of an independent Ireland without the English. With England adopting an alien political system in Protestantism (acting the ideological role that Russia did in 1916), the conventional powers of Europe, Pope-inclined, were intent to bring her down. It was essential that all of Gaelic Ireland, and this impudent Shane O'Neill, should accept English ways; firstly English political and legal ways; and by implication the doctrines and practice of the reformed and Protestant Church of England. Men like Shane O'Neill were faced not only with the extinction of

Gaelic Civilization, but with eventual spiritual isolation from the Catholic Church, an essential part of their lives.

If the Gaelic earls had to reject the Pope and be faced with everlasting Hell, it would be worth a fight. England viewed Shane O'Neill's intentions with fear and malice. Even at the time of the Wars of the Roses (1399-1485) England had been faced with invasion through Dublin, as well as Yorkist plans to invade from Calais. Lambert Simnel had been crowned King of England and Ireland in May 1487 in defiance of Henry VII, who later captured him to wash out his kitchens. England was also aware that Gaelic antipathy to the local Anglo-Irish regimes favoured foreign intrigue: the Anglo-Irish earls were an increasing burden upon their Gaelic subjects; this cemented Gaelic faith in the old ways, and provided a spring-board for the career of men like Shane O'Neill and later his brother Hugh O'Neill, to fight England over the land issue, and Protestantism. The Anglo-Irish quartered their armed retainers upon their tenants, and even the English Government condemned the evils arising from "coigny livery, kernety, bonnaught, cuddies*, etc. As foreign Catholic assault loomed upon the England of Elizabeth I, England made up her mind quickly whom she distrusted: England distrusted the Anglo-Irish, the Gaelic earls and the Church of Rome, and a hostile Scotland in the north, armed from Europe, and making intrigue across the North Channel into counties Antrim and Down, and perhaps arming the O'Neills of central Ulster, to burn up England's energy in suppressing Irish revolt.

Shane O'Neill was revolting against England's policy of the "Surrender and Re-grant" of native land, which had dated back to the laws of Sir Anthony St Leger. St Leger had advised Henry VIII to assume the crown of Ireland in 1541: the Kingdom of Ireland lasted until the Act of Union in 1800, and it outlived the

---
*
coigny - favoured position
livery - allowance of provender for horses
kernety - accommodation for light-armed Irish footsoldiers
cuddies - fighting Irish louts or vagabonds

fall of the Gaelic world. The career of Shane O'Neill coincides with one of the many Gaelic revivals. Ireland was now alienated from Gaelic Scotland; Scotland would follow the English path of Protestantism, and Scots Protestantism would soon replace the Catholic Plantations of the sixteenth century in Antrim and Down. In December 1541 the O'Neill's had "submitted" to Henry VIII, accepting a "Protestant" as King and head of the Catholic Church in Ireland; they promised to hold their lands by knights service to the Crown and to attend Parliament: instead of "The O'Neill" they received the title of Earl of Tyrone. In theory, in English law, they were as good as English lords, but in the eyes of their subjects, Catholic and Gaelic, they had made a mistake, trying to preserve their position when they should have been taking up arms like men. Conn O'Neill, primitive Gaelic earl of the north, could be seen at Greenwich near London on 1 October 1542, bowing to the Crown and accepting his new Earldom, knowing that the title would go to his eldest, but illegitimate son, Matthew. English law dictated Primogeniture succession, whilst Gaelic law favoured the claims of his other adventurous son, Shane. Shane O'Neill, of fierce Gaelic temper, and a liking for strong drink, would not brook the English law, and desired to lord it across Ulster as the Great O'Neill, the Lord of the North and the bane of the English; he wished to flout the power of the new "heretic" Queen Elizabeth I with impunity. The submission of the Gaelic earls was effective even in Tyrconnell in present-day Donegal, although the O'Donnells did not receive the title of "Earl of Tyrconnell" until the accession of James I in 1603. Like the France of Louis XIV, the Tudors found that the best way to break Irish power was to enervate it: like the later French aristocracy, the Gaelic earls were invited "to come to Court", not as in the France of Louis XIV, to play on swings in the Gardens of Versailles, but to take up Court positions, where they would learn the arts of gossip and fashion: the Earl of Desmond was educated at Windsor and was known as "the Court page". But most of the Gaelic earls would not seriously bow; and England realized that the old established policy of assuming to hold sovereignty over all of Ireland would in the end lead to Ireland becoming an independent state allied with Catholic Europe, or searching after the Gaelic dual monarchy dream.

The O'Neills were regarded by most of the other Gaelic earls as rightful Kings of Ireland, and, if a situation arose where England could be weakened, the Scots could be brought back into the Gaelic fold: an *imperator Scottorum* - an emperor of the Scots - might restore Catholicism and bring the heretic Queen to heel, with help from the Pope. To the Reformation world, England seemed a doomed country, torn apart by an alien faith, with the rest of Europe uniting against her. Her only friends seemed to be the petty German states and the Low Countries, that accepted the Protestant heresies. Europe looked back at the Catholic Church's effectiveness in dealing with other great heresies: Protestantism might last a few generations, maybe one hundred and fifty years, but it would end with Holy Mother Church's inevitable triumph. The infamous Tudor dynasty, that had started with "Henry Tydder", as Richard the Third had derisively styled him, would be long forgotten. The fate of Protestantism would be no different from the Arianism and the Pelagianism*of the Ancient Church, or the Lollardism of the Middle Ages; all these heresies enjoyed a long life and the Papacy was confident that she could bluff Protestantism out. All efforts were now made to get rid of the English "Communist" regime on the fringe of Europe - that threatened to become a world power - and to re-establish conventional religion and the *status quo*. It was essential, as far as the Papacy was concerned, that as much of the British Isles should remain as Catholic as possible: Ireland became the obvious stronghold of the faith, geographically separate from England, as Scotland fell under Calvinism.

The rash demands of Shane O'Neill, fighting for what he regarded as his rightful lordship, would lay the foundations of the utter defeat of the Gaelic World and the firm establishment of the Church of England throughout Ireland. But the people would not

---

*Long-lasting beliefs that claimed that established Catholicism was in error.

85

spiritually submit, and became entrenched as Prebyterianism, a form of Calvinism, took root during the Protestant Plantation of Ulster in the seventeenth century. The period of the O'Neill wars in Ulster is therefore an important demarcating line in Irish history. The Catholic and Gaelic past was defeated; the modern religious troubles, which have characterized Northern Ireland since the Protestant Plantation of James I, took root in the organizations and traditions that grew up around it. Religion, by the time of Henry VIII, was to further aggravate a process of alienation that had taken place between the Scots and Irish at the time of the Bruce invasion. It was to further complicate the power struggle that had taken place since very earliest times in Ireland between the north and the south. The north was also a great seat of all-Irish power and all-Gaelic power in the British Isles. It had also been a great seat of learning, as rich, if not richer, than the monasteries of the south: Armagh had three-thousand scholars when the Normans destroyed it in 1202 It was an unusual situation for the south of Ireland to have precedence over the north under the Anglo-Irish Earls of Kildare, who upheld the authority of the English Crown. The struggle in the north was at first purely local under Shane O'Neill; but under Hugh O'Neill it escalated into an all Irish struggle. By the time of Hugh O'Neill's attempt at independence between 1593-1603, the Desmond family had been defeated in the south-west of Ireland, and the ancient Kingdom of Munster had fallen directly into English hands, despite help from - Spain. It was up to Ulster to make a final stand.

Shane O'Neill claimed lordship over Tyrone, Armagh and Derry: at first he did not claim to rule all of Ulster, but his coming fight against Elizabeth put him in mind of an all-Ulster Gaelic dream, with alliances with old Dalriada in Antrim and the O'Donnells of Tyrconnell in their mountain strongholds. As far as Gaelic law was concerned, all any O'Neill or any other Irish chieftain could rule, was a whole body of vassal septs, who elected them "The O'Neill" or "The Desmond". Each chieftain had his own domain, whilst the large body of peasants held their own land, and were generally unwarlike. The chief's domain was generally quite small, in O'Neill's case being limited to a few castles, which included ancient Dun severick, seat of the Dalriada Sea-Kings. In Gaelic-ruled Ulster and the rest of Gaelic-ruled Ireland, it was the chieftain who was entrusted with ruling the people's land;whilst in feudal England, and the imposed feudal Irish system, it was the King who bestowed land and privilege. Thus Shane's illegitimate brother Matthew was regarded as an "English lackey". The peasants glorified Shane as "The O'Neill", and did not bat an eyelid when Shane slew his half brother upon Conn O'Neill's death in 1559. It was said by the English that "No subjects have more dreadful awe to lay violent hands on their lawful prince than these people have to touch the persons of their O'Neill's". As far as Shane was concerned he had lawfully killed the usurper of the sacred O'Neill title, whilst in English law he had murdered his half brother and should therefore be regarded not only as a common criminal but as in rebellion against the Crown. The Anglo-Irish, Norman-descended, could accept either law. Shane O'Neill boasted: "My ancestors were Kings of Ulster, and Ulster is mine, and shall be mine". After Shane had buried his father he summoned his clansmen to his island fort on Lough Neagh. Here in the traditional fashion he tossed a silver slipper over his head and declared himself to be "The O'Neill" to the hosts of his warriors. He commanded the allegiance of the Maguires, MacMahons, O'Reillys and other chiefs. But his biggest mistake was to alienate the Scots MacDonnells of the Glens of Antrim, who often veered to the English. It has been said that Shane O'Neill was the most resolute and most cunning of England's opponents. Certainly he started as a handsome man of fine Gaelic address. There was the element of the Greek in him, and he was sneakingly admired by the equally byzantine Elizabeth I. But drink and sexual excess were a great liability to Shane O'Neill. It was said that the Great O'Neill, after a heavy drinking bout, would often bury himself lengthwise in sand; this would counteract the effects of his terrible hangovers and bad temper.

SHANE O'NEILL

Shane had a considerable reputation as a Gaelic chieftain: he was the bane of the English in Ulster, always a thorn in Elizabeth's side, who always planned his capture. He became known as Shane the Proud, with his retinue of hired gallowglasses, wielding their mighty axes, as they had done throughout Ireland since the Middle Ages. Having helped to drive back the Normans, they had now the Tudor Monarchy, transformed into an English and Protestant one, to cope with. Shane would pitch his tent anywhere, with the great King-Candle before it, thicker than a man's body. English attempts to capture Armagh, once Shane had declared his independent hand, were soon thwarted. The Lord Deputy of Ireland, Sussex, sought terms, but Shane was ever aware that Sussex was only buying time. Shane was not surprised when a contigent of English, whom Sussex had applied for, were marched into north-east Ulster in preparation to capture him, Shane O'Neill, the arch-rebel. O'Neill knew when he could not stand and fight; so he withdrew his forces into the mountains. Secure behind the barrier of the River Bann and the broad expanse of Lough Neagh, he busily applied to France for help, with the hope of six-thousand men.

The Lord Deputy, Sussex, however was no tyrant: he generally respected the rights and formalities of the Irish people; he had no great wish to humiliate O'Neill; but he was also aware that the English law, and not the Gaelic one, should prevail. If O'Neill was to surrender, he could at best be confined to some sort of reservation, or if events went against him, and Elizabeth turned really nasty, then he could forfeit his head. As in most political situations, a lot rested upon chance. Sussex was also aware that Ireland was now divided upon its support of Shane O'Neill: one side, as represented by the Desmonds, favoured the Gaelic Law; whilst English-inclined Irishmen accepted English Law and the "legitimate" Baron of Dungannon. The English-inclined tradition was led by the Butlers. Sussex was for compromise, but he knew that a vigorously independent O'Neill in the north would perhaps mean a more devious Scotland for the Crown to cope with. However Elizabeth was determined to have her way, and Sussex was withdrawn in February 1556, and replaced by Sir Henry Sidney. He ruled until 1571, and presided over the submission of Shane O'Neill.

It was now too late for England to turn back from the precipice of the Reformation. If Papal influences were to permanently establish independent power in Ireland, then England would be sandwiched in her Protestant stronghold, between Catholic Ireland and a Catholic united Europe. It was essential that Ireland should be Protestant and English governed. England realized the magnitude of the task of making Ireland entirely Protestant; but the major destruction of Gaelic Civilization had been brought about by the Normans: the remaining struggle was with the remnants of the Gaelic world that the Normans had bequeathed to themselves as they evolved into the English. Catholic Irishmen were starting to coalesce in the face of this latest threat to the Gaelic way of life. For Catholic Irishmen, Protestantism meant the imposition of the English religion. For sincere Catholics, England was not only taking away Gaelic Law but was also taking away Christianity. Elizabeth was the harlot and the fiend of the Book of Revelation. England, the priest exclaimed, had become a pagan power, fired with the energy and arrogance of Anti-Christ. English Law, said the priest, was the law of the Devil, but at the same time the priest was not sure if the Gaelic Law veered to the law of Christ. Gaelic efforts to gain Continental help were regarded by England as a direct affront against the new state religion. The Elizabethan state had to assert itself immediately in order to survive. However English policy at grass roots level in Ireland seemed to be tempered with moderation: gone seemed to be the days of Norman barbarism. Protestantism, although it was burning Roman Catholics in England, was more tolerant towards "Papists" in Ireland; so O'Neill himself was rebelling with the possibility of success.

In 1551 Shane O'Neill, openly in rebellion against Elizabeth, had been summoned to London. The Protestant regime was open to compromise. He stayed in London from January to May 1562, at the instigation of the then Lord Deputy, Sussex. Shane O'Neill, haughty chieftain, wore a saffron mantle that swept about him in great folds. He wore long hurling black hair. As he entered the Council Chamber he was followed by a band of two hundred warriors: their heads were shaven, wolf skins flung over their shoulders. O'Neill and his warriors were a menacing sight to the culture-loving courtiers. O'Neill's warriors wore the old-fashioned leaf mail from head to shoulders and carried a three-foot battle axe in front of them. The general idea was that Elizabeth should acknowledge O'Neill's power, provided he submitted to the Crown. It is said that the Gaelic world was now surrendering; but O'Neill knew that "the submission" was but a formality, since the remains of Gaelic culture, and O'Neill's power, was left unscathed; he hoped that it could live side by side with England. Shane let out a great howl in front of the throne, like a great Red Indian chieftain confronting an American General, making his submission, throwing himself flat before the Virgin Queen. He spoke in Gaelic, of which a rough translation survives: "It was his right, being the certain son of Bacach, born of a legitimate woman, to take the succession, and that Matthew was the issue of a locksmith of Dundalk married with a woman named Alison, and not withstanding had been deceitfully supposed by his mother Con to be her son, to the end falsely to take away the dignity of the O'Neill". Few of course could understand Gaelic: O'Neill was making his point because of the striking nature of his appearance at Court, and for the simple reason that Matthew had been slain by O'Neill: the matter of the succession was therefore no longer in doubt. O'Neill hoped that Elizabeth would let him keep the title of "The O'Neill" in return for his loyalty to the Crown. Gaelic despot and English despot were very much alike: Shane, fighting for his independent kingdom, and Elizabeth fighting for her Crown against Catholic

Europe. Both were rebels of a sort, and both had much to gain by coming to agreement. It had been at Elizabeth's instigation that O'Neill had submitted in Gaelic; for O'Neill himself spoke fluent English. Shane O'Neill, former Queen's rebel, was now recognized as "O'Neill the Great, cousin to Saint Patrick, friend to the Queen of England, enemy to all the world besides". O'Neill himself, always looking forward to the next drink, was a good actor. He could lay on the Gaelic act thickly, to an equally unbelieving Elizabeth. Behind closed doors he was not disturbed, and in his cups quite flattered, that he was called "the Grand Disturber". Protestant Law, for the happy O'Neill, did not seem so bad after all. Elizabeth was not excommunicated until 1570. However Shane's title was only unofficial: his so called "submission" had gained time for both parties. Both Shane and Elizabeth realized that confrontation was inevitable. The historical progression was for the Gaelic world to be reduced, and crushed, by the power of England.

Shane returned to Ulster as "Lord of Tyrone". Meanwhile he had undertaken to expel the Scots of Antrim, who were led by Sorley Boy MacDonnell. Sorley Boy ruled from North Antrim, holding secure in the great Dunluce Castle. Dunluce protrudes into the heavy seas of the northern coast of Antrim, a castle out of a fairy-tale. The Scots were to be Shane's greatest enemy, and in the end were to be his downfall. The new Lord Deputy, Sidney, pronounced that "Lucifer was never puffed up with more pride or ambition than O'Neill is. He continually keepeth six-hundred armed men about him and is able to bring into the field one-thousand horsemen and four-thousand foot. He is the only strong man in Ireland, his country was never so rich or inhabited, and he armeth and weaponeth all the peasants of his country, the first that ever did so of an Irishman".

O'Neill was no military genius: he could not arm Ireland against England for long. He was byzantine and crafty. A few glasses of Gaelic wine, firing his imagination, could wring more concessions out of Elizabeth than an army of gallowglasses. He was full of more talk than irrevocable deeds, perhaps explaining why he could lead England a chase. A more serious armed opponent would have perhaps been defeated more quickly. He fast became, no doubt by design, a curiosity to the Elizabethan Court. Shane had compelled Sorley Boy MacDonnell to surrender Dunluce Castle in 1565, threatening to starve the inhabitants, keeping Sorley Boy prisoner. O'Neill now embarked upon two years of undisputed power. He was able to boast to Government envoys that "I care not to be an earl unless I be better and higher than an earl, for I am in blood and power better than the best of them (the new Irish earls accepting English titles), and will give place to none but my cousin of Kildare for that he is of mine house. My ancestors were Kings of Ulster and all Ulster is mine and shall be mine". Every day it is said he put away the first fish from his table for the poor. It now appeared that a good deal of Ulster was his, for Shane had defeated the Scots at Glenshesk near Ballycastle on 2 May 1565. Shane now ruled most of Ulster east of Donegal, to which he turned his attention, defeating their chieftain, Calvach. Calvach died in 1566 and was succeeded by his brother Hugh Duv. O'Neill was now striding across Ulster with unwieldly arrogance, provoking Elizabeth all the time. Perhaps an ever-increasing taste for the drink impelled him forward to a Gaelic doom. A lifetime of drinking may have instilled within him a death wish, or fired him with even greater visions. It is said that the Great O'Neill had no designs for a united Ireland or had an especial dislike of Protestantism, greater than any other Catholic princes of his times who had to live with it. The overthrow of the O'Donnells meant that Shane O'Neill had strode into Connaught. England was determined to put him down and had conspired with Calvach O'Donnell, but not before attempts had been made to poison him. O'Neill realized that Elizabeth now seriously planned his death: he could either establish a military position against England, which he knew to be impossible for any length of time; or he could fall back upon the mercy of the Antrim Scots, and Sorley Boy MacDonnell, whom he had defeated and imprisoned, but later released. The English attempted to seize Derry, which stood between northern Donegal and the lands of the O'Neills. The attempt failed, inspiring O'Neill with confidence. He marched into Donegal but he was completely routed on the banks of Lough Swilly by the O'Donnells. In a panic he fled out of Donegal and into the Glens of Antrim, making his way to Cushendun, in mind that he had released Sorley Boy, head of the Antrim Scots. Disarrayed by failure, the Great O'Neill may have morbidly taken to drink. But Elizabeth's spies were still at work. The Lord Deputy had an assassin at the banquet held at Cushendun, to which Shane the Proud was invited. Supposedly Shane O'Neill and Sorley Boy had made it up, and were uniting in the face of England. But Shane feasted and drank too well, and memories of past enmities with the Scots were short. When the drink had worked the infidel, a drunken brawl developed. The English assassin ran his sword through the insensible O'Neill. It is said that his body was carried down the Antrim Coast to a nearby monastery at Glenarm, and that it was later taken away by his followers. Meanwhile the English cut off Shane's head, the assassin hastening to Dublin Castle to receive a thousand marks from the public treasury. It was 1567, and Sir Henry Sidney felt that he had presided over the last of the Gaelic chiefs. The example he would make of the Great O'Neill, now that he was in possession of Shane's head, would deter the rest of Ireland and establish fear for the English Law. Shane's head was tarred and stuck on a pole. It was then placed on the north-west wall of Dublin Castle for all to see. Gaelic Ireland would not take fright, for Protestant England was now faced by the power of Roman Catholic Spain.

Throughout the Shane O'Neill drama the Papacy had not regarded England as fully beyond redemption. Although the practical situation had been that of open rebellion against Rome, without little possibility of returning to the fold, Elizabeth had not been excommunicated until 1570. The Papacy waited for some time before making an official pronouncement. By 1570 England, as far as the Roman Catholic Church was concerned, was now officially Protestant and without the Christian fold. A clear division had arisen between Ireland and England: future political struggles saw religion complicating matters, if on many occasions religion was not the active cause of disputes between the two islands. There had been little in the Anglican creed that the Papacy could reject, since Anglicanism was regarded as an ambiguous Christianity anyway. (It of course ceased to be a form of Christianity after Elizabeth's excommunication). When Elizabeth refused to acknowledge the Pope as Head of the Catholic Church, refusing to compromise the position that Henry VIII had bequeathed her as Protestant *Fedei Defensor*, then the break with Rome was inevitable. It would be followed by military action against England. The Protestant Dublin Parliament declared that the lives of all priests were to be forfeited: priests were to be hanged, disembowelled when half dead and their heads, like that of Shane O'Neill, to be displayed as a warning for would-be Romanists, in some public place. Anyone harbouring a priest or entertaining desires for a return to Rome were state enemies: they were to be hanged and their estates confiscated. As usual the writ of England did not run the length and breadth of Ireland. With Continental threats looming, it was essential that this should be so; and that both the Anglo-Irish and Gaelic factions should be brought to submission. If need be they should be crushed, to gain this pressing end. But in Ulster, and the Desmond Kingdom of the south-west, Roman Catholicism was openly practised.

THE SPANISH ARMADA

With the name of O'Neill legally extinguished, his lands could be shired. A new English-inclined Earl of Tyrone, a more amenable O'Neill was appointed. The English were not intent upon utter extermination of Gaelic traditions or families. Hugh O'Neill, cousin of Shane O'Neill, was brought to Court, a future

Lord of the North, who would receive an English, and of course, Protestant education; and learn English arts of war. The struggle of Gael against English for the moment left the north, and centred around the south-west province of Munster. From earliest times Munster had contact with Spain across the Celtic Sea: it was from here that some historians think the first Christian missions may have reached Ireland; and it was from here that the Gaels claimed their origin, calling themselves the Milesians. During the Middle Ages there had always been a lively trade between the south-west of Ireland and the northern and western coast of the Iberian Peninsula. In Spain and Portugal, "the noble Irish", as they were called, obtained more privileges than the Anglo-Normans. Ships plied the waters between Cork and Valencia, setting sail across the Spanish or Celtic Sea; this route became as important as the North Channel link between north-eastern Ireland and western Scotland. The Spanish Sea has ceased to be so important in modern times, perhaps because of the rising power of England, and because of the declining political power of the Iberian Peninsula; but perhaps most of all because of the geographical distance between Spain and south-western Ireland. However many Portuguese became mayors of Irish towns in the south-west; the Italian financiars, the Ricardi, Friscobaldi, the Mozzi and the Bardi of Florence became agents in Medieval Ireland. Great was the wine trade: Bordeaux, Dordogne, Lisbourne, and St Emilian were ports with Irish populations and a lively trade with an island that lay hundreds of miles across stormy seas. During modern times Ireland, especially the south, became isolated under England, whilst the north continued its traditional contacts with Scotland and the north of England. The exotic traditions and lives of the south-west peninsula and the Mediterranean-like ports of Cork and Kerry were neglected. They lived in another world, different from the Irish midlands and from Ulster. The south-west had its fascinating inns, and ports that pirates were apt to frequent, like the pirate ports of south-west England. The men of Cork and Kerry, in the Kingdom of Munster were bronzed and sun tanned;

95

whilst the subjects of the lords of the north, and the ancient men of Dalriada, were more Nordic and northward looking. In Cork and Kerry, and in the Galway and Limerick region, men looked to Spain and Portugal, and to the Italian Papacy, the direct opposite of everything Protestant.

At the close of the Medieval world, the Irish Catholic Church, under assault from Protestant England, took refuge in Spain and Portugal, Italy and in the Low Countries. In Europe, the old lazy Catholicism was replaced by the evangelizing Catholicism of the Jesuits, to counteract the efficiency of Elizabethan Protestantism. The ruling House of Munster, the Desmonds, were fervent Catholics, who ruled from Smerwick in the Dingle Peninsula. Witnessing the fate of Shane O'Neill in the north, the Desmonds were convinced that their own land titles would soon be in question. In 1568 the Desmonds were under weak leadership: they surrendered their lands, and Elizabeth was paid her feudal dues. The Brehon Laws were suppressed and the poets, celebrated in Gaelic tradition, were ostracized: the poets' "ditties and rhymes in commendation of exhortations, rebellion, rape, and ravin do encourage lords and gentlemen". The Earl of Desmond's cousin, Sir James Fitzmaurice, took up the cause of the Gaelic south-west. He was elected their Captain. Meanwhile the exiled Catholic, Mary, Queen of Scots, was looked to for leadership: the Pope was still regarded as the rightful suzereign of Ireland; perhaps Scotland and Ireland could again unite, as at the time of Brian Boru and Robert Bruce, to combat the Anglo-Saxon. To Catholics, the English were now throwing off the mantle of Christianity, and were on the verge of complete apostacy. Mary, Queen of Scots, was the captive of Elizabeth I, and still claimed to be heir to the throne of England. Fitzgerald tried to obtain Spanish help, but got none from Philip II; so he made peace with Sir John Perrot, the Lord President of Munster in 1573. The help of Pope Gregory XIII was forthcoming; but the small expedition of a thousand men was re-directed by its opportunist leader, Stukeley, to join Sebastian of Portugal against the Moors. James Fitzmaurice Fitzgerald's attempts were doomed to failure. He himself could only scramble a hundred men in a last ditch effort: he was killed in a local skirmish in southern County Limerick. The English Government declared that the Earl of Desmond's brother, John, was behind the plot, and Desmond was declared a traitor. As rebellion spread to Leinster, a force of eight- hundred Spaniards landed at the Desmond Castle of Smerwick. This was Philip II's contribution to uprooting Protestantism from the British Isles, but the English campaign in Munster was described as horrific. The poet, Edmund Spenser, who had large estates in the south-west, wrote that " ...ere, one year and a half, they were brought to such wretchedness as that any stony heart would have rued the same. Out of every corner of the woods and glens they came creeping forth upon their hands, for their legs could not bear them; they looked like anatomies of death, they spake like ghosts crying out of their graves; they did eat of the dead carrions, happy were they if they could find them, yea, and one another, soon after, insomuch as the very carcasses they spared not to scrape out of their graves; and if they found a plot of watercress or shamrocks, there they flocked as to a feast for the time, yet not able to continue there withal; that in short space there were none almost left, and a most populace and plentiful country suddenly made void of man and beast".

Advanced military technique, like other assaults against the Irish, in the end decided matters. The Tudors blasted away, with their artillery, at the Desmond castles. The Irish were disorganized, and foreign help was lukewarm. By 1586 Munster was "planted", the Desmonds losing 574,628 acres. A good deal of the land could not be effectively confiscated, as was later to obtain in the north, so that the ordinary Irish still remained as feudal vassals, ever ready to foment rebellion, and more conscious that they had lost their Gaelic heritage. A new civilization dominating them, made the Gael strive after a new form of Irish unity, other than tribal confederation. The Roman Catholic Church, with its system of hierarchy soon stepped in to provide a leadership that the English were effectively destroying in the Gaelic earls. The Irish peasant saw his native Gaelic earls return from England, like Hugh O'Neill in the north, English-educated, and fighting for Irish land, looking back to a Gaelic heritage, that the poor crofter alone seemed to be heir to. The Anglo-Gaelic landlords and the truly English landlords started to fight over the land that under Gaelic Law would mostly be peasant owned.

· The Spanish Armada came in 1588, the first great modern Continental threat against the power of England. The Irish may now have looked to Spain to be ruled by Philip II. The great flow of Irish exiles into Europe helped to back up Philip II's effort: here was a Spanish Empire, friendly to Ireland, upon which "the sun never set". Spain acted the same dominating role in Europe that England played in the nineteenth and early part of the twentieth century. The sound of an Irish accent, by the time the Spanish Armada sailed from Lisbon at the end of 1588, was common to European ears. The Irish were intriguing at the Court of Philip II, to firstly overthrow England and Protestantism as a consequence. Philip was not over impressed by Irish appeals, since he was aware that the Irish had always been lukewarm towards any foreign occupying power. Philip II would not be manipulated by Gaelic eloquence. Would a Catholic Spain be any more welcome than Catholic England had been before Henry VIII? To Spain the struggle in Ireland, north and south, was purely political, and to do with the land, with religious overtones secondary; whilst the Armada, about to be launched against England, stemmed as far as Spain was concerned, from very clear religious motives: to overthrow Protestantism and the Protestant League in Europe. Irish efforts to persuade Philip II to invade Ireland, establish an Irish Monarchy, then invade England, fell on deaf ears. Philip may have understood his Irish history; but he made a serious mistake in thinking that ships built for Mediterranean seas would be suitable for battle in the rough seas of the English Channel. Philip was resolved that any attempt to establish Spanish power in Ireland would end in failure - firstly

98

because of the lack of local enthusiasm, and secondly because of England's strategic position, and thirdly because of the distance of Spain from Ireland. Both England and Spain, in an age of expansion westwards, realized Ireland's strategic position *vis-à-vis* the Atlantic and the New World.

England thought that Ireland was Philip's objective. On the eve of the Armada there were only one-thousand eight-hundred troops in the whole island, and defences in England were also in a bad way. English troops in Ireland were usually supplemented by Irish mercenaries. Philip II may have made a grave misjudgement in his decision to send the Armada up the English Channel, instead of to the south-west Irish ports, and along the west and north-west coast - which were still largely out of English jurisdiction. Thousands of Gaels could be temporarily organized to cripple England's Irish power. Spain may have been afraid that the information she received about Ireland was unreliable and that English defences were better than the Irish made out. Philip obviously thought that it was feasible to invade England from the English Channel, striking at the south-east coast of England and at London. Spain, like England, shrank from relying upon the Irish clans, who repelled unity. The Spanish fishing fleet was off the western coast of Ireland in great numbers, with quite large ships of around a hundred tons. In 1572 Sir Humphrey Gilbert reported from Munster that there were about six hundred or more fishing off the Irish coast. So Spanish captains would have first hand information about Irish waters. Despite Spain's connections with Ireland, she did not seem to use this knowledge; nor did the two countries at grass roots level ever draw close to one another. Sir John Perrot,Lord Deputy shortly before the Armada, outlined in detail the position: He said that Leinster "stands in reasonable good terms for quietness, save for stealths and robberies which are sometimes committed"; in Munster "most of the doubtful men there are in hand, so that the state of that province is reasonably well assured, unless it be disturbed by some foreign attempt"; in Connaught "the quiet of the province is doubtful, for that they are men disposed to stir and disturbance, and ill affected to the state of the time". But in Ulster "some of the potentates there have put in pledges (to the Crown), and some not; yet they are not to be accounted as men assured indeed, but rather a demonstration and show of assurance, for that they are people light and inconstant".

In Ireland news filtered through slowly over six weeks, that the great Armada had been dispersed in the English Channel, and that the Spaniards had miscalculated. The English were chasing the Spaniards up the North Sea and around the north of Scotland. The Spaniards hoped to make for Spain by steering well off the west coast of Ireland, into the Atlantic, and then drive south for Spain, and home, with their half-wrecked ships and poor food supplies. But bad maps and navigational errors were to bring the Spanish hulls into deadly contact with the spiky coast of western Ireland. Ship after ship struck rocks as winds and gales drove them onto the shores of the Irish clans. It was early autumn on the Atlantic Coast of Ireland. The ship-wrecked sailors had little idea what reception they would receive: some like the Mayo Burkes sheltered the Spaniards, others slaughtering them as they came ashore. The Spanish numbers were great, and the English Government acted pitilessly: orders were sent for the execution of all Spaniards caught: the Irish Sheriff of Clare executed ten-thousand Spaniards, and a small number of Irish sailing with them, were wrecked and slaughtered off the west coast of Ireland.

Only in Ulster were the Spaniards assured of a more definite welcome. The O'Neills of Tyrone and the O'Donnells of Donegal were growing closer together in marriage alliances, and the state of Ulster continually worried England. Reports came in that two-thousand Spaniards were camping within six miles of Strabane; it was feared that the large numbers of Spaniards might side with the Ulster clans in their internecine feuds. English spies reported in the Killibegs region of Donegal that there were "Three of the Spanish ships coming into the harbour ... in the McSweeny country, one of them was cast away a little without the harbour, another running aground on the shore break to pieces. The third

100

being a galley, and sore bruised with the seas, was repaired in the said harbour with some of the planks of the second ship, and the planks of a pinnance which they had of McSweeny". Only one of the Spanish ships, the *Girona*, eventually managed to stay afloat, whilst as many as a thousand Spaniards surveyed and explored the surrounding countryside. The *Girona* was between seven hundred and eight-hundred tons, and about one hundred and fifty feet long. It was estimated that about one-thousand six-hundred men went ashore, a serious threat to England, considering the English standing army to be in the region of one thousand eight-hundred men. England would take no chances, even though it seemed that the Spaniard's primary task was to head for Spain, and to save one's neck. On 26 October 1588, repaired and ready for sea, the *Girona* slipped out of Killibegs harbour shortly before dawn. It was thought that the *Girona* was worthy enough to carry the Spaniards to the northern isles of Scotland; from there they would make their way inland and to the east coast of Scotland, perhaps taking better ship for Spain.

It was to be the last voyage of the *Girona*. She would find her resting place wrecked on the spiky rocks of Antrim Dalriada. The sea was too strong and too unknown for the frightened Spanish as they sailed around the coast of Donegal. Two days later the *Girona* was wallowing in rough seas. When she was off the mouth of Lough Foyle the rudder went; by now they were close to another Armada wreck, the *Trinidad Valencera*. The *Girona's* sailing had gone, so she drifted off course, driven by the wind into the rugged coast of Antrim, rolling wildly from side to side, as darkness gathered. She drifted on past and present-day Portrush, past the treacherous Skerries Rocks and the quicksands in that region. Now she approached Benbane Head. A reef struck out from the headland, and the *Girona* foundered just before midnight. She was demolished almost at once, spilling her cargo and treasure on the sea-bed, later recovered by divers in the 1960's. It was one of the most spectacular of the Armada wrecks. The sea was furious and the tide pulled the dying men towards Scotland.

They were only a few hundred yards from shore. Out of one-thousand three hundred who had left Killibegs, only nine survived. The *Girona* had come to grief near a little cove near the Giant's Causeway. The cove is still called *Portnaspanaigh,* "the port of the Spaniards".

The Scots Sorley Boy MacDonnell was resident at Dunamayne Castle, some miles down the Antrim Coast: he rescued wine and cannon from the wreck. Now at the age of eighty, having run the gauntlet between supporting the English or siding with the O'Neills, he had become definitely anti-English. One of his castles had been burned down on Rathlin Island: his wife and youngest sons, together with about six-hundred people, had perished in the massacre. He held strong at Dunamayne and at Dunluce in command of about two-thousand Scots, winning recognition for his position from Elizabeth I. In return he paid lip service to her as Queen. The English threatened Sorley Boy with death if he did not give up the hostages from the *Trinidad Valencera* and the *Girona.* He managed to procure their escape to Scotland across the ancient route of the North Channel. The Ulster chiefs were an honourable exception to the policy of rapine and slaughter in the other Irish clanships. 130 - 140 ships had perished on Ireland's western coast, from the Antrim Coast in northern Ulster, to the Dingle Peninsula in the far south-west. Philip II's plan to invade England and to re-establish Catholicism had failed. It did not deter another rising of the O'Neills in the north. The ensuing revolt of Hugh O'Neill, the English-educated Gael, and a child at the time of Shane O'Neill, was to be the beginning of the end of the Gaelic world.

TRIBAL CONFEDERACY

The struggle in the north now took on an Irish dimension. Hugh O'Neill, Earl of Tyrone, cousin of Shane O'Neill, had none of the weaknesses of his eccentric kinsman. He employed English methods of war against the forces of Elizabeth. His forces were regular troops fighting against English trained infantry. A vague sense of "nationalism" had been born. O'Neill, leading Ulster would avenge the enormities of English rule in Ireland. On his many hunting expeditions throughout Ulster, he had in mind the primitive bows and arrows of the peasantry. He would show modern guns, demonstrating their usefulness; all this in front of the eyes of the English. Legend has it that Hugh was handsome, had great wisdom, understanding, and was noble in deeds. There was also "Red Hugh" O'Donnell of Donegal. O'Donnell was brought up on the banks of Lough Swilly by the MacSweeny clan. England was determined that the rise of another powerful northern clanship should be cut off at its roots. The Lord Deputy of Ireland, Sir John Perrot, an illigitimate son of Henry VIII, sent orders that a ship should anchor in Lough Swilly opposite MacSweeny's great stone castle, under the purport of selling wine. The Irish were invited aboard, and along came the fourteen year-old Hugh O'Donnell. English soldiers sprang from the bowels of the ship, releasing MacSweeny and his followers, but taking the young O'Donnell to Dublin. He was imprisoned in the Birmingham Tower. After three years he attempted to escape, but was retaken. At last he achieved success on Christmas Eve night 1591. It was a dark and snowy evening and the jailors were full of Christmas cheer. He, together with some relations, escaped to the Wicklow Mountains: food was scarce and "Red Hugh" O'Donnell was forced to eat winter leaves. They slept in the snow, O'Donnell himself surviving, at last being found by Gaelic soldiers. "Red Hugh" O'Donnell was sent north to O'Neill, and then to Fermanagh, where he sailed in state down Lough Erne; then he went to Ballyshannon in Donegal. Here he was hailed as "the O'Donnell". Hugh O'Donnell's chief allay was therefore Hugh O'Neill of Tyrone.

O'Neill became intent upon uniting Donegal, Fermanagh and Sligo, which were traditionally O'Donnell territory, along with his own territories of central Ulster, and to form a confederation embracing Antrim and Down. Elizabeth regarded herself as "Countess of Ulster", so O'Neill's plans trod on her own pride. The familiar Tudor policy, copied from the Normans, of diplomacy backed up by Irish-supported troops, was employed. It was not as yet practical to employ a large English force against O'Neill's thousands; so like other Gaelic chieftains who had won a temporary position *vis-à-vis* the Crown by threats and deeds of violence, O'Neill was invited to London. In 1585 he had sat in parliament as Baron of Dungannon; in March 1587 he was recognized as Earl of Tyrone; but his authority rested upon Anglo-Gaelic connections, and English troops were permitted to garrison his lands. Elizabeth suspected that Ulster might inevitably make a last stand, because of its geographically isolated position as the last stronghold of the Gaelic earls: its southern borders were guarded by a long chain of lakes, forests and mountains. The Antrim Coast was ungarrisoned by English troops, so the anicient channel between north-western Ulster and the Hebrides was again open. The citizens of Glasgow supplied O'Neill's men for the coming struggle. Catholic Ulstermen and Catholic Scotsmen were united in a final stand that started to bear the stamp of a religious struggle. Most of Ireland was ruled by the Anglican Church. It was essential that there should not be a Papal stronghold, and a Gaelic stronghold, in the north.

The English attacked the reaches of Lough Erne between 1592-94 in an effort to break the southern borders of the Northern Kingdom; but English numbers were small, less than a thousand men. The English were beaten near Enniskillen in August 1594. The small clanships asserted themselves under Hugh O'Neill, who took the field in 1595: he was now openly in rebellion, and the English sent two-thousand veterans from the Netherlands. O'Neill was castigated as "the principal and chief author of this rebellion and a known practiser with Spain and Her Majesty's other enemies". Although England's troops had normally been small in Ireland, authority had always been assured by the existence of Irish mercenaries: good pay and rich booty were the rewards that

104

tempted many Gaels to win battles over their countrymen for England. Hugh was aware of all the odds against him as he assumed the sacred title of "The O'Neill", finally arousing Elizabeth's wrath and an uncompromising determination to conquer Ulster and to integrate it with the rest of the English system in Ireland. During a short truce O'Neill was in communication with Spain, asking for six-thousand soldiers. It was suggested that the Archduke of Austria should be sent to be King of Ireland. O'Neill exhorted the other Irish chieftains to rise up in defence of "Christ's Catholic religion". Meanwhile England had organized herself for full scale war. There was now seven-thousand English troops in Ireland.

O'Neill however had started off as the Government's protégé: he had served on Elizabeth's side during the Munster Wars; but as always self-interest and mercenary instincts dictated matters. His diplomacy was English; instead of slaying his cousin Turlough, rival for the O'Neill leadership, he persuaded him to give it up peacefully; in actual fact Turlough, in mind of the magnitude of the coming struggle, may not have wanted the title. As far as Elizabeth was concerned, O'Neill was motivated purely by self-interest: at one moment, if circumstances dictated, he could betray the Gaelic Confederation of the North, bringing it firmly within the English orbit; or he could firmly make a stand. O'Neill was English-educated and his support for the Gaelic cause, unlike that of Hugh O'Donnell, was political with religious overtones, and not heart-felt. Shane O'Neill may have been a drunkard, but he was a real Gael, though English-speaking The Gaelic world perished when Shane O'Neill's head was cut off at Cushendun. This new rebel O'Neill accepted, if it suited him, all English trappings, and Elizabeth, in her quieter moments, may have thought him more amenable than the barbaric but amusing Shane.

Up till 1585 O'Neill had been content to be Earl of Tyrone, an English title; but now he was "The O'Neill", which meant everything to the Gaels. He may have considered that Elizabeth would eventually throw him to the wolves, using him as Earl of Tyrone to eventually establish effective English power throughout Ulster, bringing about the fall of the O'Donnells of Donegal, and eventually dispensing with the Anglo-Gaelic earls she had created. O'Neill felt himself under threat: the loss of his lands meant for his supporters the destruction of Gaelic Ulster. In August 1598 the English commander Sir Henry Bagenal was beaten by O'Neill at the Battle of the Yellow Ford. England's increased military presence had counted for nothing. The Irish clans gathered firmly round "The O'Neill", and this English-educated Gael perhaps became the first Irish Nationalist of modern times. Camden said that "Since the time the English first set foot in Ireland they never received a greater overthrow, thirteen stout captains being slain and over fifteen hundred common soldiers". O'Neill had now twenty-thousand troops at his command. By the end of 1508 they had swelled to thirty-thousand. Once more the spectre of Spanish aid, or invasion, aiding an independent Ireland, haunted the Protestant Queen, as she entered a bad tempered old age.

The Munster Plantation of the south west rose in rebellion and was swept away. As usual the Irish lacked artillery, and it would not be possible to take the all important walled towns. Hugh O'Neill was aware that his thirty-thousand men approached the war in tribal manner, despite his exhortations; Red Hugh O'Donnell, itching for revenge at his imprisonment in Dublin during childhood, was to prove a rash and blundering ally. O'Neill basically wanted to consolidate his own position, and find an excuse to compromise with Elizabeth, in an effort to secure his land. O'Neill was favoured by James VI of Scotland, supposed to have Catholic sympathies though a Protestant. He would soon be James I of England. Help from Spain was verbal, and Elizabeth, in her old age, but infatuated by the young Earl of Essex, decided to bring matter to a head, and rid Ulster of the intransigent O'Neill. The Earl of Essex arrived in Dublin on 15 April 1599, with six-thousand foot and one-thousand three-hundred horse. Bad food supplies and an unlucky campaign in the

South, reduced Essex's strength to four thousand by July 1599. Sickness and disease, and mutiny, took their toll on his forces. O'Neill was now fighting for the demands that he had set before Elizabeth in 1596 at a time when the King of Spain had written to him, declaring that "I have been informed you are defending the Catholic cause against the English, that this is acceptable to God is proved by the signal victories which you have gained. I hope that you will continue to prosper; and you need not doubt but I will render you any assistance you may require". O'Neill's demands had stated in 1596 what the twentieth century might have called Home Rule:-

> "*That* the Catholic, Apostolic and Roman religion be openly preached and taught throughout Ireland by bishops, seminary priests, Jesuits, and all other religious men.
>
> *That* all cathedrals and parish churches, abbeys, and other religious houses, with all tithes and church lands, now in the hands of the English, be presently restored to the Catholic Churchmen.
>
> *That* the Catholic, Apostolic and Roman religion be openly preached and taught throughout Ireland by bishops, seminary priests, Jesuits, and all other religious men.
>
> *That* all cathedrals and parish churches, abbeys, and other religious houses, with all tithes and church lands, now in the hands of the English, be presently restored to the Catholic churchmen.
>
> *That* there be erected a university upon the Crown rents of Ireland, where in all sciences shall be taught according to the manner of the Catholic Roman Church.
>
> *That* the Lord Chancellor, Lord Treasurer, Lord Admiral, the Council of State, the Justices of the Laws, and all other officers appertaining to the Council and Law of Ireland, be Irishmen.
>
> *That* all statutes made against the preferment of Irishmen, as well in their own country as abroad, be presently recalled.

That the Queen nor her successors may in no sort press an Irishman to serve them against his will.

That O'Neill, O'Donnell, the Earl of Desmond, with all their partakers, may peaceably enjoy all lands and privileges that did appertain to their predecessors two-hundred years past.

That all Irishmen may freely travel and traffic all merchandises in England as Englishmen, paying the same rights and tributes as the English do.

That all Irishmen may freely build ships of what burden they will, furnishing the same with artillery and all munition at their pleasure...."

FLIGHT OF THE EARLS

In 1599 Elizabeth preferred that Essex should execute a campaign north immediately. Essex wasted the English effort, and incurred the wrath of Elizabeth. Essex made a truce with O'Neill. He was recalled by Elizabeth on 24 September 1599. He was executed by the headman on 25 February 1600. Lord Mountjoy arrived to mount a new campaign in February 1600 with an army of twenty thousand, knowing that Hugh O'Neill ruled more of Ireland than the Queen of England. There was no possibility of compromise with O'Neill; Elizabeth was hysterical in her old age and moaned that Mountjoy should never "pardon the arch-traitor, a monster of ingratitude to her and the north and the root of misery to her people". Mountjoy's plan was to hem O'Neill in to his fortified Ulster, turning O'Neill's greatest asset against him, cutting him off from his southern allies. A fort was erected at Derry, cutting off communication between the O'Neill and the O'Donnell lands. South-west Ireland (Munster) gave out under sustained attack; and O'Neill was left in Ulster, guarding the Gap of the North and hemmed in behind his trenches with about four-thousand men. O'Neill had a price on his head, for which would be given £2000 alive and only £1000 if dead. Some of O'Neill's supporters were induced onto the English side when they saw the scales weighed against him. Sir Arthur O'Neill was brought over, and Niall was offered the Earldom of Tyrone. Help was at last forthcoming from Spain, but the fleet containing four thousand men, sent by Philip III, instead of heading for some northern port, probably Lough Swilly, landed at Kinsale in Munster, a province that England had reconquered. It was 23 September 1601. Mountjoy now marched to counteract the Spanish forces; and O'Neill in turn marched south after him with an army of twelve thousand. The Irish and Spaniards could not act in unison, and Mountjoy won the day, the Spaniards surrendering at once. O'Neill hurried north to make his final stand amongst the wilds of Tyrone - as tradition has it, the last of the Gaelic earls.

Mountjoy destroyed the inauguration stone of the O'Neills at Tullahoge, near Dungannon. Meanwhile "Red Hugh" O'Donnell had taken ship for Spain, to beg a new army in 1602; but it is thought that he was poisoned by an English agent. The Great O'Neill was on his own, and the increasingly maniacal Elizabeth triumphant. Only Mountjoy's tactics shone; for neither Hugh or Elizabeth was there personal satisfaction or victory. In Tyrconnell famine and desertion weakened O'Neills western flank, whilst the same malignancy spread into Tyrone. The O'Donnells submitted to the Government. O'Neill was lucky that in Mountjoy - though a cruel and determined soldier - lay a humane and just diplomat. If O'Neill had held out longer his people might blame him for the terrible famine that swept the land, or his fear of punishment for political misjudgment. An English observer said at the time that there were "multitudes of ... people dead with their mouths all coloured green by eating nettle docks, and all things they could rend up above the ground. These and many like lamentable effects followed their rebellion, and no doubt the rebels had been utterly destroyed by famine, had not a general peace shortly followed Tyrone's submission ..."

Tyrone was reduced to a bandit, hiding around the Lough Neagh region, whilst Elizabeth's troops scoured the hills for him. It was only three months into 1603 when O'Neill had had enough and emerged a beaten and degraded man from the woods. He arrived at Mellifont Abbey on 30 March 1603, disarmed and finished. No doubt he had been on the verge of starvation. Mountjoy realized that if he himself had been beaten by O'Neill he would be perhaps standing in some place equally degraded. Upon submitting and entering the room, he prostrated himself, grovelling upon the earth, his features lined and beard grizzled. Whilst the English were now content to let O'Neill keep his head - which he must have realized before making a submission - they were determined to keep him humiliated. The Great O'Neill, former Lord of the North, was forced to kneel before Lord Deputy Blount for one hour. On 1 April he was made to submit to the Lords of the Irish Council, and then he was taken to Dublin on 3 April: he submitted to the representatives of the Irish Parliament. Throughout his acts of submission O'Neill was deprived of vital information about a key event that had taken place in England. For on 24 March 1603 Elizabeth I died, aged 70 , and James VI of Scotland had become James I of England. Throughout the submissions O'Neill was full of emotion, and his submission to Elizabeth was a very personal matter. Mountjoy had tricked him; for O'Neill, to save face, could have submitted to James - which he was later forced to do. The English observer Moryson said that upon hearing of being tricked, and of Elizabeth's death O'Neill "... could not contain himself from shedding tears, in such quantity as it could not well be concealed, especially in him, whose face all men's eyes were cast ... the most humble submission he made to the Queen he had so highly and proudly offended, meant nothing, if he had held out till her death".

The Irish, and their mercenaries, who had fought against the Crown were now permitted to leave Ireland over the next few years. O'Neill, despite being tricked, was reinstated to his earldom under James I. The death of the Gaelic world had ended with the familiar policy of "Surrender and Re-grant".O'Neill's enemies in the Government were many. The Gunpowder Plot came in 1607. O'Neill, to save his life, decided upon flight. A ship pulled in at Rathmullen Harbour in Lough Swilly under French command. O'Neill would go to various places in Europe, to Brussels, the King of Spain, and when all these failed, to the Pope in Rome. O'Neill made his way north, where he stayed two nights at Dungannon Castle, no doubt looking out at the green hills and breathing in the air of his home for the last time. He was a deeply disturbed man. In his morbid moments he perhaps would rather wish death that the life of wandering and exile that lay ahead. Amongst the humiliations was his promise not to solicit the aid of foreign powers:he had been forced to write a letter to the King of Spain that must have stung his heart. It was now 1607. O'Neill journeyed to Lough Swilly, now that England had decided to strip him of his lands and titles, marked out for a Protestant Plantation. He had with him his wife Catherine and some attendants, and the O'Donnells. Ninety-six persons are said to have boarded the French ship in Lough Swilly. The ship left little Rathmullen, sailing into the cold North Channel and down the coasts of Scots Protestant Antrim and Down. The ship headed south for the Mediterranean. They had a stormy voyage, putting in at the Isle of Man. At last they landed in France, short of provisions. Rejected at many European courts, the Pope at last granted O'Neill a pension in Rome. Once England had learned of "the Flight of the Earls", English spies were active, waiting to see if he would engineer a return to his sequestrated Earldom. He might try to arouse the wrath of Catholic Europe. O'Donnell died in 1608. O'Neill lasted until 1616, without hope of return, and perhaps without desire. He was given a royal funeral and he was buried in the Franciscan Church of San Pietro di Montorio on the Janiculum Hill.

THE PLANTATION OF ULSTER

In Europe it was not only Ulstermen and other Irishmen that were refugees: this was the of refugees fleeing from religious and cultural persecutions, from one European country to another. English Puritans went to the New World, and of course to Ulster. Irish upheaval between the accession of Henry VIII in 1509 and the death of Elizabeth in 1603, was part of a general European hysteria. The age of the Counter-Reformation had dawned; it was the age of displaced minorities. Hugh O'Neill was not alone in his flight to Rome, said to have been the most popular city of refuge, in a world that was steadily being divided between Roman Catholics and Protestants. The pilgrims who now went to Rome had little prospect of returning to their native land. The world of Hugh O'Neill was without hope. Refugees from Catholic countries started to make their flight in Europe from the 1540's to Rome or London, if one was a Catholic or Protestant respectively. As the Catholics were fleeing out of Ireland, the Protestant Huguenots from the massacre of Saint Bartholomew in 1572 were coming in, chiefly to Dublin, and to the Lagan Valley and Belfast region in the north of Ireland. The main refuge for converted Catholics was Switzerland, particularly Geneva, where Calvinism, to which Ulster Presbyterianism traces its roots, had its origin in the late sixteenth century. For many, real sentiment for the home country was forgotten within a generation, and memories of past persecutions, faded with time. But Owen Roe O'Neill, a descedant of Hugh O'Neill, together with other displaced Catholic Irishmen, would not forget about their Gaelic past so easily.

The Southern Netherlanders were a nation on the move as well, the Protestant north and Catholic south of the country taking shape amidst great strife. In the British Isles, the Scots were on the move to the Baltic countries: it was estimated in 1620 that there was in Poland about thirty-thousand Scots of Catholic persuasion. It was an age of universal barbarism, which the fate of the Gaelic world in Ireland only reflected. Religious quarrels and ideology had come to complicate the issue of land confiscation in Ireland. Confiscation of Gaelic lands would perhaps have taken place anyway if there had never been a Reformation or a Henry VIII. It was a world of dispossessed petty rulers, who scavenged abroad, the luckier ones like O'Neill, gaining a pension of the Pope. They were condemned to oblivion, running up against restrictions on citizenship of the towns and lands that they had adopted. Refugees were forbidden to buy houses without special permission of the authorities. Often the destitute Gael or Catholic of Ulster, would find himself socially and culturally persecuted by the Catholic countries he had fled to. He had been dispossessed for what the modern mind would call racial reasons. The vast bulk of the Irish peasantry remained: but other countries like Spain succeeded in doing a complete racial purge: the heathen Moriscos from Granada were scattered throughout the Iberian peninsula, later to be expelled altogether. Irish Gaels held land that the English Crown always wanted; so even if men like O'Neill might have embraced Protestantism, they would most likely have suffered a similar humiliation. Between the death of Elizabeth in 1603 and the death of Cromwell in 1660, England succeeded in ridding Ireland of the English-educated Gaelic ruling classes, some of whom had embraced Protestantism, and some like the Earls of Antrim had managed to remain Gaelic and Catholic, whilst supporting the Crown. Men like O'Neill had put themselves out on a limb in the face of Protestant England; whilst men like Antrim managed to survive to ape the new ways.

The period 1550-1660 witnessed the decline of the Papacy and the Catholic Empires that had enjoyed undisputed primacy. To the Catholic world the heretic established his position and was carrying Protestantism to America. Protestantism would take over the whole of Ireland. The Presbyterians, fired with Calvin's visions, flocked into Ulster from the Scottish Lowlands under orders of James I. As a child James had disliked the Presbyterians, and perhaps welcomed their migration from his native Scotland.

The Catholic world was in economic decline and unable to defend its position against the rising commercial north of Europe. Ireland, Spain and Italy faced the assault of Protestant nations, and England aspired to take over the role of maritime Spain. France was to linger on as a "low" Catholic country, that had almost gone Protestant in the late sixteenth century at the time of the Huguenot massacres. Political uncertainty prevailed in Europe: Islam threatened to destroy Europe internally. Markets were suffering. Economic uncertainty caused greater investment in land: in Ulster and the rest of Ireland, as the plantations went under way, the English and Scots took over the role of the overthrown Gaelic landlords, shiring the country and establishing English Law: a disorganized and unarmed Gaelic peasantry confronted them, without help of an O'Neill and despised by the remaining Catholic Anglo-Irish, concerned with their own positions. The land was as important an issue as religion. Religion was to become an overriding issue in the centuries ahead. England had now made Gaelic Ireland leaderless, until a new Anglo-Gaelic peasantry threw up leaders like Mr de Valera and Michael Collins to ape the role of the O'Neills and the Desmonds in a twentieth century democratic arena. The seventeenth century was an era of bloody religious wars, fought on the ruins of late Medieval economic issues: The Thirty Years War in Germany wiped out one third of her population . The religious quarrels and murders that were to rend the Protestant Plantation of Ulster apart, were firstly the inherited problem of the confiscated Gaelic lands; and secondly, the twentieth-century aspect to the problem - the religious divide, that opened up as a result of the policies of the Anglican Church, and the hysteria engendered by Puritanism and Presbyterianism. The decadence of the Catholic world had reared up these problems. The victory of England over Spain by the time of the Armada in 1588 could be likened to a victory that the Soviet Union might gain over the United States, and the grave cultural and ideological problems which would arise. Scots and English planters entered Ulster to take possession of the land, acting the role of soviets and regarded as usurpers by Catholic Europe. The Protestants were regarded as against civilization, advocating the rule of the Devil instead of the rule of the Pope. Protestantism, whether its Anglican established brand or Presbyterianism (its anti-Establishment brand), felt threatened by what most of Europe considered was the legitimate power of the Catholic Church and the established powers of kings (the English were to behead theirs).

The Scots Protestant Plantation of Ulster had clear economic motives: there were no serious evangelizing attempts made on the Gaelic Catholics by the one hundred and fifty-thousand Lowland Scots and about twenty-thousand English. They occupied the lands of the Great O'Neill. The economic invasion was not immediate: O'Neill had lingered on from finally submitting to Elizabeth (then to James) in 1603, until departing in 1607. In 1628 it was reckoned that there were only two-thousand British families "planted" in the six chosen counties of Coleraine, Tyrone, Fermanagh, Armagh, Donegal, and Cavan. County Monaghan was left to the Irish; whilst Antrim and Down had already large numbers of Highland Scots by a long tradition. As the Plantation developed, Protestants identified more with Counties Antrim and Down, having had long connections with the north-west of Scotland and the Lordship of the Isles. From the beginning the Anglican Establishment, and the rival Presbyterian creed, lacked moral political authority amongst Roman Catholics. Few of the English and Scots settlers spoke Gaelic, which was the dominant language; only the Gaelic aristocracy were biligual. Remaining Gaelic earls like Lord Antrim tended to keep themselves to themselves if possible and only serve the triumphant Anglican power if really forced to do so. Francis Bacon advised the Crown that the Gaels were too primitive to accept the new religion and that the Gaelic version of Roman Catholicism was even more pagan than the apostasy of Rome herself. Gaelic Civilization had been in decline for five-hundred years: Protestant fear saw the Devil, dressed like the Pope, holding out in the bogs and moorlands of Fermangh and Tyrone. The degraded condition of the Gaels was proof of Protestantism's - especially Presbyteriansm's - great mission. Protestantism (so its many variants believed) was the true apostolic faith of Christ. Feelings between Roman Catholics and Protestants were mutual: Anglican ritual was dubbed "the Devil's service". Roman Catholics could be seen crossing themselves when Protestants were near in the event that anti-Christ might possess their souls. To the Protestant, the priest was a Druid in disguise: the Gaels should be confined to reservations, on the poorer lands, like later American Red Indians.

Many believe that Irishmen would have sunk into this severe poverty by 1600 whether England influenced events or not. But the world of the Great O'Neill is pre-industrial - a world that did not exhibit the industrial and social and economic problems of a later age. In an agricultural civilization, Ireland, England, Scotland and Wales had as much chance of individual success as any other European countries. Irishmen point out, and certainly men like Hugh O'Neill believed, that English influence stunted Irish potential. Englishmen, with a knowledge of history, remembered that at the retreat of the Romans, the Irish had invaded parts of Britain: England's conquest of Ireland was reversing a situation that the Irish might have attempted on the same scale in England, given the numbers. The Ulster Plantation, like all the previous plantations of the sixteenth century, started in an atmosphere of siege. The poor Irish had suffered as a result of both the aristocratic Gaelic and aristocratic English conflict. The Catholic Bishop, David Rothe wrote in Cologne in 1617 that the Irish "have no wealth but flocks and herds, they have no trade but agriculture or pasture, they are unlearned men, without human help or protection. Yet though unarmed they are so active in mind and body, that it is dangerous to drive them from their ancestral seats, to forbid them fire and water: thus driving the desperate to revenge, and the moderate to think in terms of taking arms. They have been deprived of weapons, but are in a temper to fight with

nails and heals, and to tear their oppressors with their teeth ....
Since they see themselves excluded from all hopes of restitution or
compensation, and are so constituted that they would rather
starve upon husks at home, than fare sumstuously elsewhere, they
will fight for their altars and hearths, and rather seek a bloody
death near the sepulchres of their fathers thanbe buried as exiles in
unknown earth".

Contemporaries relate that Irishmen lusted after every sin,
now leaderless and having lost their identity. It was said that
murder and incest were everyday crimes. Sir Henry Sidney had
said that "matrimony among them is no more regarded in effect
than conjunction between unreasonable beasts". As in the troughs
of the Norman period, cattle raiding, violence and tribal warfare
reigned supreme. To eradicate this was the problem posed in
Ireland, especially in Ulster, which the English reckoned would
still be most intransigent even though the earls had fled.
Englishmen made the mistake that Ireland could be made like
England, by letting Roman Catholicism remain unevangelized,
whilst Roman Catholics started to believe that Ireland could never
be Ireland, or Ulster part of Ireland, unless all Irishmen became
Roman Catholics; or accepted a Roman Catholic state.

O'Neill had not been suddenly driven out by the English in
1603: the number of chiefs had only been reduced, not destroyed:
O'Neill could go on as an English earl; but he obviously
considered this to be unviable; he could not possibly survive as an
overthrown Gaelic king, since he had claimed to be "The O'Neill".
O'Neill had received generous treatment of James I, but there had
been officials hostile to him. O'Neill thought that he might be
brought before the Irish Council on charges of conspiracy and end
up losing his head. It was perhaps this overriding fear that led to
his flight on 14 September 1607. It was perhaps a course of action
that the English Government expected him to eventually take.
Deprived of real power, and suspected of fomenting rebellion, the
Gaelic earls would conveniently discredit themselves. Ulster now
became an American Virginia on the door-step of England. At

117

the close of 1607, O'Donnell and his supporters were indicted on charges of conspiracy: O'Neill was to lose his civil rights by act of attainder and his lands were confiscated to the Crown. In Irish Law, O'Neill was only the guardian of the peasants' lands, the peasants themselves being proprietors. The Irish peasant was now reduced to his landless, lord-dependent, English counterpart. Several of the minor chiefs rose in rebellion, in Armagh and Fermanagh, their lands confiscated or "escheated" to the Crown and their civil rights denied. O'Doherty rebelled and marched on Derry, but was slain. Some of the beheaded chieftains spent up to twenty years in the Tower of London.

The "Articles of Plantation" were issued in May 1609, throwing some half a million acres of profitable land out of four millions of acres open to Scots and English settlers: they undertook to perform services for the Crown in return for holding estates of one-thousand, one-thousand five hundred and two-thousand acres. These "Undertakers" were to lease out their lands to "Servitors", who were mainly Lowland Scots and Presbyterians. The Crown admitted the impossiblity of the task; for the third rank of settlers were the great bulk of "Natives", who had to inevitably employ the native Irish: the "Native" settlers were not required, like the "Undertakers" and "Servitors" to take the Oath of Supremacy, acknowledging the King as Head of the Church. The Lord Deputy, Sir Arthur Chichester, felt that the amount of land confiscated was too great and that at least half should be left to the native Irish; but Puritanism was not open to compromise. The Established Church was well endowed. The Anglican Trinity College, Dublin had been established in 1592; whilst land was also set apart during the Plantation for Royal Schools in each of the new shires or counties: the Royal Schools were Mountjoy (1614), Portora (1618), Armagh (1621), Cavan (1621), Banagher (1629), Clogher (1632) and Donegal (*circa* 1632). These however were Anglican dominated, for Presbyterianism as yet was only organized within the Established Church.

118

The term "British" was now applied to the new Scots and English planters. Towns that had fallen into decay during the rebellions, like Carrickfergus and Coleraine, were reorganized. Nineteen new boroughs were created, all under strict Anglican control. The City of London was granted all the lands between Coleraine and Derry - lands of thick woods and teeming fisheries. The Protestants went hunting and trapping, building their log cabins in a New World atmosphere. However in was in southern Antrim and County Down that the Scots capitalized on their already existing centuries of connections, which was to eventually form the spearhead of the Presbyterian effort. The Presbyterians were economy-minded, like all planters, but they kept themselves to themselves more than the Anglicans: the Presbyterians gradually aroused the suspicion of the Anglican Establishment, and the extra special loathing of the Catholics. The Presbyterians, more Bible-based than the Anglicans, were very anti-Pope. The Presbyterians formed a community within the Ulster Plantation, eventually accused of bigotry, because of their strict Puritan ways; they were persecuted by the Anglicans because they denied episcopacy: James I, in mind of his childhood fears of them, had said "No Bishop, No King": for Anglicans, Presbyterians were Republicans at heart and as potentially rebellious as Roman Catholics.

The English-designed fortified manor house safeguarded Protestant rule. The "Big House" of the Scots-English north was different from the already existing Gaelic castles of Ulster and from the "Big Houses" of the south of Ireland. Ballygally Castle, five miles from Larne on the Antrim Coast, was built as a large stone dwelling house, surrounded by a protective bawn, between 1625-6. It was built for James Shaw of Greenock, who came across the famous North Channel route. The new Scots and English manors competed with the prevailing Gaelic structures. At Ballygally, the Scots Shaw's Castle guards the glens. It stands at the left hand of Ballygally Bay; whilst the ruins of Cairncastle (O'Halloran's Castle), erected on a huge rock protruding out from

Ballygally Head, and at the right hand of the bay, looks out into the sweeping headlands of Antrim Dalriada. It views most of the North Channel and the island realms of Scottish Dalriada. Sloping up from Scots Ballygally Castle lay the fields of the planters, whilst the Catholics inhabited the higher regions and enclaves of the glens. The head planter's mill lies a mile up the back road from Ballygally Castle and its associated dwellings, lying outside the castle walls. Angle turrets and conical candle-snuffer roofs survive at Ballygally Castle - sited around a small river, essential as a water supply. The river runs through the lord's gardens, within the protective walls. The Shaws would keep regular contact by ship, afforded anchorage in the deep and sheltered Ballygally Bay, with their kinsmen in Greenock. In the twentieth century their castle has gone through several extensions to become a hotel. Ballygally Castle is particularly Scottish. The larger English magnates built Jacobean mansions like Joymount (1610) at Carrickfergus and Charlemount (1622-24). Both these have been destroyed; whilst the smaller, and some very beautiful structures like Ballygally Castle, have survived Ulster's troubles.

Outside of the restricted, but prosperous, planter life, lay the walled towns like Londonderry, capital of the Plantation. Londonderry had a population of about three thousand in 1700; whilst Belfast, apart from Sir Arthur Chichester's Castle, had only about six-hundred inhabitants. Like Londonderry, Belfast had its corporation and port trade. Belfast would soon compete with Londonderry, that became increasingly isolated: at its foundation Londonderry was ideal for trade with Scotland, lying only fifteen miles from the Scottish coast; Londonderry had obvious strategic importance. But Scotland was a declining kingdom; whilst Belfast was ideally situated opposite the rising and commercial power of Protestant England. Internal communications within Ulster were poor, divided into clan-infested routes under command of the Gaels; and the planter roads, hacked out through the forests and mountains, and dangerous in this pioneering land. A major road was built between Belfast and Derry; otherwise communications

120

were safest and most efficient by coastal traffic.

There remained a large middle-ranking Gaelic aristocracy at large, and a large labouring class of Gaels after "the Flight of the Earls": the Protestants could never effectively occupy all the Gaelic lands even though only twelve and a half per cent out of four-million acres had been earmarked. The New World attracked most other colonizers, but many contemporaries said that the Ulster or American pioneers were wicked men who had left behind the errors of their ways in England and became extra special Puritans abroad. They watched the policy of "Surrender and Re-grant", which had gone on for centuries in Ireland, again persued. In County Down, Magennis of Iveagh, was re-granted all his twenty-two thousand acres: in 1623 he was created Viscount Iveagh. The Gaelic earls, who were re-granted land, started to accept the English system, and they were regarded as lackeys by the labouring classes of Catholics. The foundations of "nationalism" had been laid amongst the peasantry.

However, by 1641, the process of confiscation of Gaelic lands had gone forward. Out of the four-million acres in the six counties (excluding Antrim and Down), Protestants now owned three millions; but much of this land, because there were not enough Protestant settlers, was still occupied- though not owned under English Law - by Catholics. The large Catholic minority in Ulster was assuming a modern form. The apparent success of the Ulster Plantation inspired similar efforts elsewhere in Ireland, and Munster was again planted. The Gaels were degraded; but the planters were not much better. The historian Reid said in his *History of the Irish Presbyterians* that "Among those whom divine Providence did send to Ireland ... the most part were such as either poverty or scandalous lives had forced hither". A son of a Presbyterian minister said at the time that "From Scotland came many, and from England not a few, yet all of them generally the scum of both nations ..." They fled from debt and justice . Dispossessed Gaels, and desperate planters striving to establish a political position (and a new religion), were to provide

121

fresh fuel for future conflagration.

Mountjoy, who had defeated O'Neill, described the new planter stock: "Because the Irish and the English-Irish were obstinate in Popish superstition, great care was thought fit to be taken that these new colonies should consist of such men as were most unlike to fall to the barbarous customs of the Irish, or the Popish superstition of Irish and English-Irish, so as no less cautions were to be observed for uniting them and keeping them from mixing with other that if these new colonies were to be led to inhabit among the barbarous Indians".

THE GREAT REBELLION

The Lord Deputy of Ireland, Sir Arthur Chichester summoned Parliament. Parliament sat between 1613-1515: unlike the English Parliament, Catholics were not barred: a Protestant majority was manufactured, chiefly by the creation of thirty-nine new boroughs and by the influence of the local sheriffs. The political struggle that typified later centuries had taken shape out of economic issues and religious differences. The Catholic representatives were tame and confirmed the confiscation of O'Neill's estates, and confirmed the Plantation of Ulster. Unlike the Tudors, the Stuart Dynasty was not fond of parliaments, because of the growing financial problems of the Monarchy: it was a Medieval institution existing at the start of the problems of the new Capitalist Age. The King preferred to be independent of Parliament and to raise his . own finance. Money-based, the House of Commons tended to challenge the Divine Right of Kings - the theory that the King was God's anointed and that the King stood above the Law. The tendency was both in England and Ireland to do without Parliaments. The pro-Parliament Party of the House of Commons became focused around the Puritan Movement and Presbyterianism; whilst the Church Party was the party of the King's Divine Right over elected representation, and for the subordination of Parliament. The Church in Ireland however took a much more Calvinistic line. It preferred one hundred and four articles of the Anglican faith, instead of the thirty-nine articles of the Church of England. In this way Calvinism and Presbyterianism could bypass the anti-Church laws. The principle that James I had feared, of "No Bishop, No King", became established in the breasts of Puritans. By the time of Cromwell, it infected the whole body of the anti-Church Party, which became known as the Parliamentarians or Roundheads. The Stuarts, under Charles I (1625-49) were inclined to "Popery"; and Puritanism established an English Republic by 1649.

Ulster Protestants were aware that Roman Catholics were in a better position in Ireland than in England, and were able to obtain in the Chichester Parliament the abolition of eleven of the newly-created boroughs; and were able to prevent the regular enforcement of existing laws against their religion. From the start the Plantation of Ulster was uncertain of its life; the Protestants uncertain of their dominance over Catholics; whilst the Catholics, having a relatively credible base, even after the O'Neill Wars, had a chance of establishing a position. Protestants feared that the Catholics might take over the Plantation. Catholics were aware of the English Monarchy's weak financial position. In 1627, in return for £120,000, Charles I granted them "the Graces"; amongst other liberties, it gave them permission to practise as lawyers (thus establishing the possibility of getting the laws against Catholicism substantially changed). There was also to be no interference with land titles of sixty years standing. The Puritan-inclined Church in Ireland, under Archbishop Ussher exclaimed that "the religion of the Papists is superstitious and toleration a grievous sin". There was an increasing body of Irish Protestants, especially Ulster Protestants, against the Established Church. The Puritan was anti-bishop. If there was to be no bishops, then as James I had said, there would some day be no king. The Monarchy was now determined to purge the realm of

123

anti-Church rebels and the Parliamentarians. Sir Thomas Wentworth was created Lord Deputy of Ireland in 1632 and in 1639 Lord Lieutenant and Earl of Strafford. A man of German-like efficiency, he became hated, as he purged the Church in Ireland: his rule of iron became known as the policy of "Thorough". Lord Wentworth himself was an ex-Parliamentarian and had changed his coat to gain high office (1633-1641). To gain money for the Crown he accused settlers in Ireland of running the country in their own interest. He attempted to rule Ireland for eleven years without Parliament. Puritanism and political opposition to the Crown had coalesced. He displeased both Catholics and Protestants alike: he denied Catholics a chance of representation by not summoning Parliament, and made Presbyterianism heretical and on a par with Roman Catholicism. Archbishop Laud, to the Presbyterians an outright Papist in doctrine, purged the Anglican Church of Puritanism. The basically ill-trained army in Ireland was re-formed into an efficient force of nine-thousand men; a direct affront against the busy planters. An efficient army would be a future threat to the liberty of Roman Catholics, who still harboured desires of a Gaelic return, and a means by which Presbyterians could be put in their places.

Ulster Scots joined with the Scots in Scotland in signing a National Covenant against Wentworth and Laud's High Church Party in 1639. War between Presbyterian Scotland and Anglican England seemed inevitable. Wentworth tried to impose the "Black Oath of Allegiance" on the Ulster Scots to ensure their support for the Crown. The Presbyterians, who had practised within the Established Church, were to establish their first presbyteries by 1642/3. Wentworth accused the London Companies in North Derry of not carrying out their obligations; he confiscated their charter, fining them £70,000 His lawyers busily searched for flaws in land titles to gain possession for the High Church Party, ruining Presbyterian interests. Wentworth's rule did much to benefit the poor, whilst the rich and corrupt, as many thought the greedy planters, were put in their places. By 1639 war had broken out with Scotland, and Wentworth stationed his nine-thousand strong army at Carrickfergus in Scots County Antrim. However the Scots and the Parliamentarians defeated the High Church Party in the British Mainland. Wentworth was summoned to London and was accordingly executed by his enemies. Owen Roe O'Neill, an Irish mercenary in Continental armies, was awaiting revenge for Shane and Hugh O'Neill. Irish soldiers, adventurers as much as the Scots planters, in the service of the Low Countries, Spain and Italy, now looked at the prospect of fighting against England for Irish soil. The prospect of good pay, and rewards in land, was embellished by the idea of patriotism, the Gaelic revival, and fighting for Holy Mother Church. Father Luke Wadding, head of the Irish Franciscans at Rome, was organizing the new resistance movement. He sought the aid of the Pope and the scheming Cardinal Richelieu of France. Rory O'Moore had co-ordinated activities both in Ireland and abroad, and plans were made for a rising in Ulster for 21 October 1641. Overthrow of the petty Gaelic landed interests had left a horde of bandits scouring the moorlands and hills; they joined hands with political and religious forces for the overthrow of the Scots and English.

The planters were caught unawares: they fled to Enniskillen, to Derry, to Coleraine, and to Belfast and to Carrickfergus, abandoning their neatly laid-out plantations, losing their farming wealth. They were under real siege now in their walled fortresses. The old Catholic families came forth, headed by the lawyer Phelim O'Neill, backed up by the Magennis, the O'Hanlons, the O'Quinns and the O'Farrells; the O'Hagans; the MacMahons, the McGuires and the O'Reillys. The thirty-thousand strong horde that threatened English-held Dublin was only two-thirds armed. In this the Puritans took hope, as they themselves took refuge in Dublin. The seizure of Dublin Castle had been prevented by a betrayal of Catholic plans. It is said that during the rising a fierce massacre of Protestants took place, greater in western Ulster (the lands of the O'Neills) than in the east. Some say at least 610,000

125

Protestants were slaughtered in all Ireland; whilst modern scholars put the figure at around ten thousand. Fearful tales of mutilation and atrocity, of both men and women, reached Puritan London, confirming the belief that Satan was rampant in Ireland and that the Pope would shortly be at the head of his legions. It is estimated that the population of Ireland was about one-million one-hundred thousand. It is certainly true that Protestant rumours at the time were exaggerated, since the Authorities themselves admitted that the number of Protestants in the whole of Ireland was about two-hundred thousand. Some authorities, writing shortly after the date of "the massacre", put the number as low as four-thousand Protestants slaughtered; whilst about eight-thousand perished as an indirect result of the following two years of rebellion. Apparitions of murdered Protestants were claimed to be seen inhabiting rivers and swamps. On the other hand the Lord Deputy, writing to the King six days after the rising, said that "They (the Catholics) took four considerable towns, and have killed but one man". The English Puritans, surrounded by the forces of Rome, France and Spain, no doubt exaggerated the massacre in order to inspire their forces with fanaticism for the coming struggle.

Catholics also claim that Protestants mercilessly slaughtered Roman Catholics. It is said that in County Antrim, at Carrickfergus and in Island Magee, Protestants slew one-thousand Catholics. They say that the Protestants within the walls of Carrickfergus Town stormed out of the walls and stripped the Catholic quarters of their inhabitants. The Protestants chased the Catholics from their homes for miles out of Carrickfergus, and into the Island Magee Peninsula. The hysterical Catholics fled up the peninsula, all the time hunted by the Scots soldiers. Island Magee looks out into the North Channel. Here men, women and children met an horrific end. The Catholics were cornered at the Gobbins Cliffs: the Puritans would have no mercy. An Irish poem says that "Oh, tall were the Gobbins Cliffs, and

126

sharp were the rocks, my woe!/And tender the limbs that met such terrible death below".

THE ENGLISH REVOLUTION

Gaelic Catholic and Anglo-Catholics in Ireland gathered forces at Kilkenny Castle on the River Nore in May 1642. This was in southern Ireland. The following war of Puritan versus Catholic, of Republican versus Monarchist throughout the British Isles, was not even to spare the lives of babes. It is said that English soldiers often tossed Irish babes upon their swords. The confederation of Kilkenny proposed a Catholic Parliament for Ireland loyal to the English Crown, with carefully defined civil rights for Catholics. King Charles I was claimed to be a friend of Ireland and the Catholic Faith. Ulster Protestants and English Protestants were now politically and religiously at the edge of a great precipice that still yawns in modern times. In August 1642 Civil War broke out in England. The Monarchy's financial difficulties had given religious factions their chance. Charles I would play with both sides in order to keep his Crown. In February 1642 Charles had accepted the Puritan Parliament's Adventurer's Act, whereby the King was forbidden to pardon Catholic rebels. The Scots were permitted to gain concessions from King's difficulties: the King, and his Parliament, bargained with the Scots. In April 1642 General Munroe landed at Carrickfergus, supported by the Ulster Protestants. Ulster Scots, chiefly Presbyterians,now allied with the Anglican Church in an effort to keep the Catholics at bay; whilst the English Purtians stirred up the Irish Catholics in the hope of overthrowing the King. The English Purtians were anti-Monarchist, unlike the Ulster Presbyterians. James I's dictum of "No bishop, no King" seemed to be only true of English Puritans; he had misjudged the Scots and Irish ones. However the Presbyterians had already formed their independent enclaves in

Ulster: On 10 June 1642 five Presbyterian chaplains of the Scottish army met at Carrickfergus to constitute the first presbytery on Irish soil. Ministers were placed at Ballymena, Antrim, Carncastle, Templepatrick, Carrickfergus, Larne and Belfast, along with several in County Down. They were backed by the Scots General Munroe.

The Irish Parliament now excluded all Catholics; whilst the Kilkenny Confederacy represented a Catholic Parliament open to Protestants and for religious toleration. Derry and Enniskillen became the refuge of fleeing Protestants who now put their hope in Munroe's army. They supported the Monarchy and the *status quo*, despite their common religious ground with the English Puritans, who under Cromwell, would behead their King. The Catholic Confederacy dithered: many Catholics still preferred to avoid conflict and secretly wished to support King Charles if some kind of toleration was in the offing. By now Owen Roe O'Neill, who had commanded Spanish armies in the Spanish Netherlands with distinction, landed in Donegal with arms and money supplied by the French Cardinal Richelieu. With O'Neill came General Preston, who represented the Old English Catholic tradition; Old English and Catholic Gaels united in the name of Ireland and the Catholic Church. Gaeldom and Catholicism were one. Owen Roe O'Neill took command in Ulster, where his uncle Hugh O'Neill had been defeated and driven out and divested of his lands, and where Shane O'Neill had been a real Gaelic King.

The Catholic army in Ulster had been disorganized under the lawyer Phelim O'Neill. Owen Roe O'Neill reorganized it to face the formidable Scots forces of twenty thousand. The Papacy, observing the Civil War in England, regarded the defeat of Protestantism - dividing the British Isles - as a foregone conclusion. The Scots General Munroe was defeated at Benburb with a force of six-thousand men against Owen Roe O'Neill's five thousand. Over three thousand of O'Neill's adversaries lay dead; two months provisions and one and half-thousand draft horses were taken. O'Neill's losses were only seventy men killed and a

128

hundred wounded. The Old English Catholics were divided within the Catholic Confederacy and over their loyalty to King Charles I. They did not co-ordinate their plans with Owen Roe O'Neill. O'Neill and his Old English allies were turned against each other, turning Catholic forces against Catholic forces. Throughout the struggle Charles's main concern was to unite all factions, Ulster Scots, Scots Puritans in Scotland, the Scots generally, Old English and Gaelic Catholics in Ireland in the cause of the Monarchy, with promises of reforms and a more tolerant Anglican Church. All efforts were made to keep the fanatical English Puritans, headed by the Bible-thumping Oliver Cromwell, from taking over the Monarchy. King Charles I was executed by the English Puritans on 30 January 1649. In August, Oliver Cromwell arrived in Ireland with twenty-thousand troops. The religious struggles of Ireland were really stirred up by the arrival of Republicanism and revolution in England. Protestants and Catholics were united in their belief that Cromwell had been high-handed in executing Charles. To kill the King was an act of anti-Christ. Ulster Protestants believed that their position would be safer once Cromwell was defeated, and the Monarchy restored. At the root of Ulster Protestantism, Puritanism, Presbyterianism and Anglicanism, lay support for the Crown. English Puritanism and anti-establishment politics was a brand all on its own, with nothing in common with the planter Puritanism of Ulster, adventurer-based. Cromwell came to Ireland fired with visions from the Old Testament. He would bring the whole of Ireland within English and Puritan power: he was an enemy to both Scots planters and Catholics alike; and this eventually forced Protestant and Catholic unity, as he came proclaiming "eye for eye, tooth for tooth, and arm for arm". Cromwell had in mind the Catholic massacres of Protestants. In early September he moved north to storm and sack Drogheda, near the border of Ulster, where three and a half-thousand people were put to the sword: he then turned south in an even fiercer massacre at Wexford. The hope of a united Irish army was dashed when O'Neill died in

Cavan on 6 November 1649.

The English Parliament appointed a National Thanksgiving Day in celebration of the massacre at Drogheda; by a unanimous vote it placed on the Parliamentary Records "That the House does approve of the execution done at Drogheda as an act of both justice to them (the butchered ones) and mercy to others who may be warned by it". Resistance to Cromwell did not end until 1652, by which time the Cromwellian army was thirty-four thousand strong.

At the beginning of the story of divided Ulster, Protestants and Catholics fought together on behalf of the Crown against an English Republic. It was a Royalist army that was slaughtered at Drogheda, made up of both religions. Cromwell left Ireland on 26 May 1650, the most hated man in Irish history. Thirty thousand of the troops that had fought Cromwell left for France and Spain, leaving defeated Ireland a desert of famine and plague. About half a million Irish perished, which was a little under half the population of Ireland. There were also transportations overseas. Many were transported to Barbadoes as slaves.

Ulster Protestants now suffered along with Ulster Catholics and the Catholics of all Ireland in the ensuing settlement. More land was confiscated, but the religious divide between Protestants and Catholics had taken such a firm root. The issue of the land was to reinforce these religious divisions in the coming centuries. The Gaelic world of independence and land had passed away; and it was a matter of religious preference for Irishmen that it was a Catholic or a Christian one. England had arrived, now a Republic, to establish a Puritanism unliked by everyone except the English. But Cromwell died in 1658. The British Monarchy returned under Charles II, in 1660. Ulster Protestants gave it their traditional support and the Catholics their traditional loathing. Ulster Protestants had sat on the fence for a good deal of the time, and had been like the executed Charles I. Only in the end, when all hope of establishing their own position was gone, had they thrust in their lot with the Catholics. But if Cromwell had have been

130

defeated, it is unlikely that the sudden alliance of Protestants and Catholics in Ulster would have lasted longer than the immediate cause. The religious issue had taken a firm root on the already existing land question, having its roots in the Gaelic world. Already existing problems, and the problems of the Modern Age, were to cement the Protestant and Catholic divisions. The modern Ulster problem had taken form, with Catholic Ireland making her last stand.

Conclusion

THE LORDS OF
THE NORTH

THE LAND

The great clans of Ulster had led rebellion against England since the appearance of the Normans in 1169: now the clans had all but disappeared. They were "clans" to the English and "kings" to the Gaels. They were Catholic landlords, looking to the Gaelic Brehon Laws, but of course accepting many English traditions in order to survive. The Anglo-Irish landlords were left, and now strengthened under the Cromwellian Settlement of August 1652. There was a small number of Old English Catholics - English landlords that managed to survive, holding to the Catholic faith, and revering the Crown. The land was an issue that transcended the Protestant-Catholic debate: it was an issue that the Gaels themselves fought over, ever since the Kingdom of Ulidia (Antrim and Down) had been submerged into Gaelic Ireland by the time of Saint Patrick. The arrival of England complicated matters; the Normans, then the Tudors and Stuarts, considered Ulster and the rest of Ireland, ripe for plantation. The English came to Ireland as they did to America. The invaders from England wanted the land; but there was an immediate cultural gap. This must have attracted England in the first place: word spread into Wales and to London that the primitive Gaels were ripe for conquest. However England found to her detriment that the land was not so easily conquered; that the Gaels had a great population, and were more stubborn in their primitiveness than the Gaelic landlords of Wales and the remnants of Anglo-Saxon power in England.

The Gaels could not govern their lands from either a central monarchy or a well-organized confederation. Tribal confederacy did not last long in the tenth century, and was not built upon like earlier efforts in Medieval Germany; perhaps tribal confederacy would have fallen asunder whether England entered the scene or not. The Gaelic lords of Ulster did not take their conquest by England lying down: some were exiled like O'Neill and O'Donnell; others preferred to be slain like O'Doherty of Inishowen, whilst many of the others preferred to be interred in the Tower of London for up to twenty years. The Gaelic earls resented England's policy, formulated by the Normans, and continued by the Tudors and Stuarts, of demanding the surrender of Gaelic land, and then its re-grant under English law. English law and Gaelic law uncompromisingly conflicted: English law demanded that the eldest son inherit property or land; whilst Gaelic law left it open to election and supposedly to the worthiest candidate. By 1700, after the religious struggles that culminated in the Battle of the Boyne in 1690, Ulster had suffered perhaps more than any other Irish province from pillaging and rapine and land confiscation, characteristic of wars elsewhere in Europe (for example the Thirty Years War in Germany).

The Normans were stern masters: they logically hoped to conquer the land and assimilate Gaelic Civilization, and to Normanize Ireland. The English emerged out of Norman culture, and were left with the problems of surrender and re-grant of Gaelic land. Although O'Neill and O'Donnell had rebelled; it was only in the last resort were the pettier earls imprisoned in the Tower. Many Gaelic lords, like MacDonnell of Antrim and Magennis of Iveagh, accepted the policy of surrender and re-grant, and survived into the twentieth century. It was a "foregone conclusion" that Gaelic land would fall under the vastly superior arms of the English Crown, fearful always of Continental menaces. England's expanding population demanded expansion westwards. Both the Normans and English who settled in Ireland, for example the Earls of Ulster, became "more Irish than the Irish themselves": to the uneducated they could be mistaken, and were often accepted, as "real Irish".

Gaelic Civilization had declined by the time of the Norman conquest; it had been shattered by the Vikings: it could hope for - and had - revivals in periods of English decline and internal monarchial dispute. Long periods of relative independence, or "home rule" were enjoyed, particularly by the O'Neills of Central Ulster. But inevitably, as English power revived, the Gaels became unwittingly united and suppressed under the power of the much larger other island. The aristocractic struggle for Gaelic land ended by the time of Cromwell, since the Gaelic aristocracy had been irrevocably diminished. A Catholic peasantry and a Catholic nationalism had been born. It did not forget the land struggles of the Gaelic earls; the peasants always remembered "the Flight of the Earls" ; a symbol of English tyranny and a symbol of Gaelic defeat, as the Gaels, the warring Goidels of old, "ran away" to Europe. Irish peasant nationalism was aware that the Gaelic earls who took flight spoke fluent English and were perhaps not as Gaelic as the romantic tended to make out. Irish nationalism emerged out of the defeated aristocratic Gaelic culture; this had itself conquered Ireland, beginning about 700 BC, reaching its peak in the fifth, sixth and seventh centuries A D.It had sharply declined under the Viking onslaught, and took four hundred years to peter out and to be absorbed into the British system. During the period 1700-1920 the English language became the Irish language; by 1920 only a handful of peasants spoke Gaelic. Today part of Ireland has political independence and land ownership by the peasantry, obtained under the English Protestant Ascendancy of 1700-1920. It is a peasant democracy, middle class and Roman Catholic-based, that has reservations about the great O'Neills and the O'Donnells, about the contribution and the role they played, defending Gaelic land, against the power of England.

The lords of the north held out longer than any of the other Gaelic earls, chiefly because of their geographically isolated position, and their long links with Scotland. In the end the suppression of the link with Scotland (since Scotland was a hostile power to England) meant the inevitable submission of the greatest of the lords of the north, the O'Neills and the O'Donnells, followed by the lesser chieftains. Once Scotland was included in the British Isles system, the Scottish link was again capitalized on to develop the Plantation of Ulster: in the end the Catholics were left with 500,000 acres out of 4,000,000 acres in Ulster. Under Cromwell out of 20,000,000 acres of land in Ireland, it is estimated 11,000,000 English acres were "planted", 8,000,000 acres of this land being "profitable". Under Cromwell, Ulster Protestants suffered the same land confiscations as Catholics, despite their common economic and political - though differing religious - ground. Cromwell hoped to control Irish land with an army originally numbering thirty-four thousand men, but which was reduced to nineteen thousand by 1655. The soldiers sold their investments to speculators, who formed a new element in the Protestant influence; this came under Anglican control with the restoration of the Monarchy: Charles II was proclaimed King in Dublin of 14 May 1660. Cromwell's followers had seen the doomed future of an English Republic and had engineered the return of the Monarchy, one Cromwell had died, and had been succeeded by his unsuitable son, Richard.

Cromwell's financiers turned to Ireland to help retrieve his debt to them: he owed "the adventurers" £360,000 and the troops £1,500,000. In Ulster, Counties Antrim and Down and part of Armagh were given over to the soldiers only. Similar arrangements took place elsewhere in Ireland. Catholics - and Protestants - who had fought against Cromwell were transplanted to Mayo, Galway and Clare. The Catholic leanings of the restored Monarchy shocked the Cromwellians and alarmed Ulster Protestants and goaded the Anglicans into action. Catholic claims for the restoration of land started to be accepted in aristocratic circles. The Act of Explanation in 1665 dècided that the Cromwellians should give back one-third of the confiscated land. The Earl of Tyrconnell, Lord Lieutenant of Ireland under the Catholic King James II, worked for a Catholic "takeover" in Ireland, and by implication, the destruction of the Protestant Plantation of Ulster. The peasant land problem, and religion, had now become inherently interwoven. With most of the land confiscated, it was the fight of Catholic Ireland, putting hope in the Catholic King James II, to secure victory over Protestantism and bring about a Catholic land settlement. This of course would only favour the Anglo-Irish earls and only a few of the more amenable, and radically diminished, Gaelic aristocracy. The

138

defeat of James in 1690 meant that Ulster Protestants were forever in possession of Catholic land.

PLAGUE AND FAMINE

In the Modern Age the Great Famine of 1845-7 was extensively documented, analysed and condemned. It was one of the many famines in Irish history. Earlier famines were thought to have been as severe, but of course are not so well documented. The famine following the Bruce invasion of 1315 was an immensely important factor in politically dividing the north of Ireland from Scotland. About half of Ireland's population perished. Bruce was blamed for the ravages of the campaign, blackening the age-old Scots connection in Ulster. The transformation of the Norman and Gaelic agricultural system into a form ready to accept Capitalism, was caused in part by the vast economic and social confusion resulting from the fourteenth-century famine and plague: these were a constant hazard that Irishmen had to live with. In the sixteenth century, famine and pestilence, following the O'Neill wars, was a factor persuading Hugh O'Neill to submit to England in 1603. Life was built around one's stomach, and the rich Gaelic lord, perhaps more than his Norman or English counterpart, could sink to the level of the peasants more easily. However ancient and medieval Ulstermen lived with famine just as twentieth century Irishmen live with religious trouble. It was horrific to witness the cattle turn into skeletons and the crops shrivel. The effects were perhaps more short-term than long-term as far as general prosperity was concerned. Like the First and Second World Wars in modern society, the shock delivered was so great that quick recovery was essential - together with some rapid advances - in order to survive.

The threat of starvation undoubtedly helped to keep Ulstermen firmly believing the Catholic faith. Fear and thanksgiving, and unbelief, after periods of calamity in a country

139

more primitive than others in Western Europe, helped to cast deep roots for Holy Morther Church in Irish soil. Protestantism arrived at a time when the Medieval system of open fields was at a close, and when the plantation and capitalist system were in their infancy. Assurance of food supply, more than in other European countries, has governed the history both of the north and south of Ireland. Cattle and cereals and fish were what men starved over and fought over in the many local wars within Gaelic society. During periods of famine, owners of land died and speculators both Gaelic, Norman and English could gain a dishonest grip.

Just as intriguing is the effect of plagues, the great ones occuring in 664 AD, at the time of the expansion of the Gaelic Church; then in 1348, after the Bruce invasion; this last plague was the infamous Black Death. All these plagues were common to other European countries, whilst the famines were not. Ireland was not however affected by the isolated plague that hit London in 1665 in the reign of Charles II. Amidst the religious upheavals, triumphant Protestantism appeared to be given a Divine blow, as London, to the Roman Catholic a new Babylon, was consumed by the buboes; then Catholic Ireland further rejoiced as fire swept the city of Anti-Christ. During periods of great natural calamity morals tended to be lax: men and women became more desperate - a situation that the Church came in to check. The plague of 664 AD may have hastened the migrations from Ulster to Scottish Dalriada; it may have developed the monastic movements, for monasteries in isolated spots like Iona, were natural havens against the plague and were less affected by famine, if their system was organized properly. However the migrations into Ulster from England and the Scottish Lowlands in the seventeenth century were not of course caused by plague; they were partly in response to the British Mainland's expanding population (firstly in the sixteenth century); then to the devastations culminating in 1607, population-wise , caused by the O'Neill wars. The Ulster Plantation was built upon the economic and political misfortures of the Gaels: famines as a result of the Scots invasion of Ireland in the fourteenth century,and the accompanying diseases carrying off large numbers. Like the famines, the plagues, whether horrific or isolated tragedies, stimulated Irishmen, and other Europeans, to recover and fare better, rather than to permanently put them down. The effects of isolated plague, for example following Cromwell's campaign, could be devastating. The historian Prendergast records that "Five-sixths of her(Ireland's) people had perished. Women and children were found daily perishing in ditches, starved. The bodies of many wandering orphans, whose fathers had been killed or exiled, and whose mothers had died of famine, were preyed upon by wolves. In the years 1652 and 1653 the plague, following the desolating wars, had swept away whole counties, so that one might travel twenty or thirty miles and not see a living creature. Man, beast and bird were all dead, or had quit those desolate places. The troops would tell stories of the place where they saw a smoke, it was so rare to see either smoke by day, or fire or candle by night. If two or three cabins were met with, there were found none but aged men, with women and children; and they, in the words of the prophet, 'became as a bottle in the smoke', their skins black like an oven because of the terrible famine".

NORTH AND SOUTH

Internal politics in Ireland, even before the invasions of the Vikings, Normans and English, followed the course of other smaller European countries: the country fell into regions and provinces: by the time England took command, Ulster emerged as the most powerful and most rebellious of these provinces. From earliest times the north of Ireland was demarcated from the south: it appears that Before Christ there were two lots of invaders, the earliest invaders in Stone Age times coming from Scotland (the Larnians); then the Gaelic Milesian race, either from Spain or Central Europe via the British Mainland. English rule merely covered up for many centuries the already existing divisions within Ireland, and the independent position of Ulster, that always came to the fore when rule from the British Mainland weakened. Munster, of course, in the south-west of Ireland, followed an independent path as well as the other smaller regions, for central government has always been a problem, or an unwanted commodity, in Ireland. Ulster, linked with Scotland, and more impenetrable than the other provinces, could do something about her particularist attitude both towards outside invaders, towards England and towards Ireland. She fell under Scots influence; the Ulster Scots persued their own interest, they had had their own differences with the Irish, differences that continued despite English interference. Relations between the coasts of Antrim and Down with western Scotland and the Highlands had been going on since earliest times.

The Scots up to the devastations of the Bruce invasion in the early fourteenth century had a more acceptable role in Ireland. The Scots Gallowglasses gained a lasting foothold in Ulster. The Gallowglass warriors helped the Gaelic chiefs to drive back Norman England. A large Scots presence in north-east Ulster was to further accentuate political divisions between the north and the south of Ireland: Ulster, before the Scots Protestant Plantation of the seventeenth century, was starting to form a colonial sphere for Scotland as well as for England. Irishmen could talk in terms of the Scots north-east in the Middle Ages. The northern Uí Neíll lords had been the *Ard Rís* or Emperors of Ireland in competition with the southern Uí Néill lords. However it had been the southern Goidel Emperors who dominated Ulster by the time of Saint Patrick (*circa* 432).

It was the north of Ireland that adopted the Ardriship, and it was in the hands of the northern lords in which in died out by the time of the Scots-Irish Emperor, Brian Boru, in the eleventh century. After this several attempts were made to create a Scots-Irish cultural and imperial sphere, to combat the power of Norman England. Any Irish success was perhaps due to Norman incompetence. Norman England threatened the Gaelic west of the

142

British Isles; but Welsh, Scots and Irish could not form a united empire. Robert Bruce in the fourteenth century was the last *Imperator Scottorum.* When Irish "unity" had collapsed at the time of Brian Boru, it was the north of Ireland, with its Scots flavour, that held sway over the south. After the English experience of the Plantation of Ulster in the seventeenth century, and the ascendancy of Protestant England (1700-1920), it was the south that gradually took over the role of the fallen Lords of the North. A middle class democracy, Roman Catholic based, emerged by 1920. England had utterly crushed the power of the northern families by 1607, when Hugh O'Neill took ship for Europe - the last of the Gaelic earls.

The rise of Protestantism gave Ulster, under Scots domination, another opportunity to persue her independent line: she took over the role of the north Ireland, forsaking the claims of the Ardris, making herself apart from the island of Ireland. Ulster sought shelter under England's Protestant umbrella from the Papal deluge. This seemed to be inevitable if England withdrew from Ireland. Ulster, to survive, has always had to assert herself against the other provinces, whether this has been under the northern Emperors or against England, or against the claims of the south at the time of the southern Emperors. Today the north-south struggle continues. It is a struggle that has re-emerged, as the power of England has receded; a struggle that was perhaps covered up when unity was artificially imposed during the Anglican Ascendancy. The dream of the *Ard Ris,* at rest at Tara, may as yet be realized. The unity of a country may not take place through established channels; its realization may be seen through a closer and deeper look into history. The assertive role of the north of Ireland, strongly under the hand of Ulster, has made important contributions, for better or worse, from the beginning of time.

The Etherow, Nr Marple,   *September 1980*
Stockport, Cheshire.

143

SELECT BIBLIOGRAPHY

1. General History

Brian de Breffny, *The Irish World* (Thames and Hudson 1977).
Brian Inglis, *The Story of Ireland* (Faber and Faber 1966).
Edmund Curtis, *A History of Ireland* (Methuen 1964).
I.J. Herring, *History of Ireland* (Wm Mullan and Son 1951).
J.C. Beckett, *Confrontations: Studies in Irish History* (Faber and Faber 1972).
_____ , *A Short History of Ireland* (Hutchinson 1973).
_____ , (Ed), and R.E. Glassock (Ed), *Belfast* (BBC 1967).
Maire and Conor Cruise O'Brian, *A Concise History of Ireland* (Thames and Hudson 1972).
Magnus Magnusson, *Landlord or Tenant? A view of Irish History* (The Bodley Head 1978).
Padraig Lane, *Ireland* (B.T. Batsford 1974).
R. Dudley Edwards, *A New History of Ireland* (Gill and Macmillan 1972).
_____ , *An Atlas of Irish History* (Methuen & Co 1973).
Seumas MacManus, *The Story of the Irish Race* (The Devin-Adair Company 1941).
Terence de Vere White, *Ireland* (Thames and Hudson 1968).

2. Earliest Times and Early Christianity

Angela Antrim, *The Antrim MacDonnells* (Ulster Television 1977)
Duncan Norton-Taylor, *The Celts* (Time-Life International 1974).
F. Marian McNeill, *Iona, A History of the Island* (Blackie 1973).
Jim Cantwell, *Holy Places of Ireland* (New English Library 1973)
John Bannerman, *Studies in the History of Dalriada* (Scottish Academic Press 1974).
Frank Mitchell, *The Irish Landscape* (Collins 1976).

Maire & Liam de Paor, *Early Christian Ireland* (Thames and
Hudson 1958).

Myles Dillion and Norma Chadwick, *The Celtic Realms*
(Weidenfeld and Nicolson 1967).

Ludwig Bieler, *Saint Patrick and the Coming of Christianity.*

Paul Walsh, *Irish Chiefs and Leaders* (Three Candles 1969).

Thomas F. O'Rahilly, *Early Irish History and Mythology* (Dublin
Institute for Advanced Studies 1967).

T.G.E. Powell, *The Celts* (Thames and Hudson 1958).

W.G. Wilson, *Church Teaching, A Handbook for Members of the
Church of Ireland* (.A.P.C.K. 1954).

Wallace Clark, *Rathlin, Disputed Island* (Volturna Press 1971).

3. Vikings and Normans

Ambrose (Rev) Coleman, *Historical Memoirs of the City of
Armagh* (Brown & Nolan/M.H. Gill 1900).

Charles Haliday, *The Scandinavian Kingdom of Dublin* (Irish
University Press 1969).

E. Estyn Evans, *Mourne Country* (Dundalgan Press 1967)..

Jennifer M. Brown (Ed), *Scottish Society in the Fifteenth Century*
(Edward Arnold 1977).

John Watt, *The Church in Medieval Ireland* (Macmillan 1972).

Ronald Nicholson, *Scotland, The Later Middle Ages* (Oliver &
Boyd 1974).

Robert Armstrong, *Through the Ages to Newtownabbey.*.

4. The Tudors and Stuarts

Aidan Clarke, *The Old English in Ireland 1625-42* (Mac Gibbon &
Kee 1966).

Charles (Sir) Petrie, *The Great Tyrconnell* (The Mercer Press 1972).

D.M.R. Esson, *The Curse of Cromwell* (Leo Cooper 1971).

Edward MacLysaght, *Irish Life in the Seventeenth Century* (Irish University Press 1969).

George Hill, *An Historical Account of the Plantation of Ulster at the Commencement of the Seventeenth Century 1608-1620* (Irish University Press 1970).

J.G. Simms, *Jacobite Ireland* (Routledge & Kegan-Paul 1969).

James G. Leyburn, *The Scotch-Irish, A Social History* (The University of North Carolina Press 1962).

Niall Fallon, *The Armada in Ireland* (Stanford Maritime 1978).

Peter Beresford Ellis, *The Boyne Water* (Hamish Hamilton 1976).

Richard Berleth, *The Twilight Lords* (Allen Lane/Penguin 1978).

Richard Bagwell, *Ireland Under the Tudors* (Holland Press, Vols I, II, & III).

_____ , *Ireland under the Stuarts* (The Holland Press, Vols I, II, & III).

Tony Gray, *No Surrender! The Siege of Londonderry 1689* (MacDonald and James 1975).

T.M. Healy, *Stolen Waters* (Longmans 1913).

Sir Thomas Phillips, *Londonderry and the London Companies 1609-1629* (Belfast 1928).

5. Society, Economics and Violence

James Hewitt, *Eye Witnesses to Ireland in Revolt* (James Hewitt 1974).

L.M. Cullen, *Life in Ireland* (B.T. Batsford 1968).

M.W. Heslinga, *The Irish Border As A Cultural Divide* (Van Gorcum 1962).

Dr William Petty, *The Down Survey* (Irish Archaeological Society 1951).

6. British and European History

Arthur D. Innes, *England under the Tudors* (Methuen 1932).

A.F. Pollard, *The History of England* (Oxford 1941).

Bede Jarrett, O.P., *A History of Europe* (Sheed and Ward 1933).

Christopher Morris, *The Tudors* (Fontana 1966).

E.L. Woodward, *History of England* (Methuen 1947).

Fitzroy Maclean, *A Concise History of Scotland* (Thames and Hudson 1970).

John Bowle, *Henry VIII* (George Allen & Unwin Ltd 1964).

G.N. Clark, *The Seventeenth Century* (Oxford 1960).

Leopold Von Ranke, *The History of the Popes* (G. Bell & Sons 1913 3 Vols.).

Philip Ziegler, *The Black Death* (Collins 1969).

R.H. Tawney, *Religion and the Rise of Capitalism* (John Murray 1926).

S.T. Bintoff, *Tudor England* (Penguin 1965).

T.E. Tout, *Edward the First* (Macmillan and Co., 1913).

William C. Atkinson, *Spain, a Brief History* (Methuen & Co 1934).

Winston S. Churchill, *A History of the English Speaking Peoples, Vols II & III* (Cassell 1967).

W.E.H. Lecky, *History of the Rise and Influence of Rationalism in Europe, Vol I* (Watts & Co 1910).

8 General Primitive Christianity

Eusebius, *The History of the Church* (Penguin 1965).

Hans Lietzmann *A History of the Church Vols I, II, III, & IV* (Lutterworth Press 1961).

Henry Chadwick *The Early Church* (Penguin 1967).

Philippe Wolff, *The Awakening of Europe* (Penguin 1968).